CRAVINGS

Why Do I Do What I Don't Want To Do?

MARJORIE COLE

Preface

There are as many reasons to explain "why I feel bad" as there are ways to deprive the body of what it needs to feel good. Poor relationships, contaminated and dead foods, the lack of minerals and vitamins, and so forth do not even begin to describe the reasons for the difficulties we find ourselves caught in. Add to these the consequences of generational sin, social adversity, difficult living conditions, anxiety, poverty, stress, and abuse, and we still have only a partial list of things that may be causing our defeat. The loss of motivation and the exhaustion that comes from disappointment and the constant drive to overcome failure strap us onto a torture wrack of endlessly trying to solve life's irresolvable conflicts.

Cravings takes us beyond the superficial understanding of addictions and our struggles to live life well by revealing the deeper context of spiritual warfare and demonic programming that operate behind the scenes in any addiction. The wide brushstrokes of coping used by many how-to and self-help books fail to paint an accurate or complete picture of recovery. *Cravings* offers more than another hypothetical new way to manage pain and torment. It gives the reader a biblical, in-depth look at the spiritual battle that goes on inside of us that makes deliverance a real and strategic part of our healing and recovery.

The first eleven chapters of the book review our spiritual condition after the Fall and the spiritual consequences of not obeying God's instructions. It also includes God's true description of who we are and what He had to do to fix us. As it turns out, the kind of food we choose to eat is far more critical to our physical health and spiritual freedom than we may have been led to believe.

This section of the book underscores both the biological and spiritual power of food and eating as they relate to willpower and our efforts to manage our own undesirable behaviors in order to overcome them. Though at first glance, eating may look like merely a physical activity that carries no moral weight or relationship to an addiction, the Bible identifies food and eating as extremely critical spiritual activities. They sit as the centerpiece on the table of choices that determine our sanity and sobriety in the battle for spiritual victory over the darkness.

Cravings takes a look at the war going on inside of me, the one that "wills to do good," and assesses the "evil present with me," (Ro. 7:21). It examines Romans 6–8 to discover the heart of the human problem is the struggle between "doing the things I do not want to do" and "not doing the things I want to do." It allows us to examine the intricate operation of our physical bodies and the interconnectedness our bodies have with our souls at a deeper level of spiritual warfare. It takes a closer look at the internal battle we are in to more fully understand how the Kingdom of Darkness has successfully invaded every place in our lives, including eating and addictions, to destroy the work and purposes of God by getting us to destroy ourselves.

At the end of many of the chapters you will find "food for thought" in the form of review questions to assist you in examining and applying the information to your own situation. We recommend you take the time to pray through them. We encourage you to read through the book carefully and let the Holy Spirit use the words of these pages to direct your hearts and minds into the victory of the finished work of Jesus Christ in your life.

Other resources to help you lay a scriptural foundation for freedom can also be found by visiting our website at **www.liferecovery.com**.

Contents

Introduction

Doing the Things I Don't Want to Do

How many of us are trapped and torn between doing the thing we hate and trying to do something different? We are determined to overcome those things that plague our lives and make us feel miserable. We fail. We try again. We fail. We are stuck, and the rut gets deeper. We become anxious and are afraid that nothing is ever going to change.

Whether the goal is to stop using or to lose weight or to be good or get better, we seem to be caught in an insidious cycle of trying harder, only to find that it is never enough. We feel guilty and angry. Our lives are becoming consumed and controlled by the very cravings we seek to manage. We are bound by addiction and are being rendered powerless.

We begin to live a mindless existence, strapped to the torture racks of Hell. Trying to manage the feelings of "I've got to, but I can't," sets us up in opposition to ourselves. We are held fast in the relentless grip of fear and frustration, dissatisfied and unhappy. Unable to do it right or to muster up the willpower to change no matter how hard we try, opens the door to failure. Anxious and driven, we search for peace and rest like someone lost in the desert looks for water. We are "like one who lies down in the midst of the sea, or like one who lies at the top of the mast" (Pr. 23:34). Armed with the negative list of our past failures, we charge ahead with a renewed determination to change.

"Wine mocks us" (Pr. 20:1), and food betrays us. *Confusion* finally convinces us all is lost and our quest to overcome is hopeless. We conclude that we have no choice but to keep on doing what we do not want to do and settle for a bondage to what we cannot seem to quit, outwit, or overcome. Agreeing with "It is what it is" sets up an ongoing agreement with and a reluctant acceptance of things we cannot seem to change. The power of past experiences convinces us that nothing will ever change, thus allowing "the way things are" to become "the way things will always be."

So, what is the answer to life's controlling habits? Is it a need for more self-discipline, greater willpower, or stricter diets? Will more faith or a stronger determination give us mastery over the cravings that seem to rule our lives in so many different and subtle ways?

For many, life has been reduced to a battle to overcome their addictions and obsessions. For others, it appears to be a call to perfection or a matter of taking responsibility. But is it lack of willpower that has rendered us helpless and has cast us into such a sorry state of distress and disgrace? Or, could it be the lack of knowledge and poor understanding that have kept us from the truth, held captive in this no man's land of hopelessness, as we continue to do "the things we hate," (Ro. 7:15)?

Whatever and however cravings present themselves, any battle to resist them ultimately becomes physically exhausting and spiritually discouraging. Not clearly understanding our foe, we attribute the internal struggle to our own flawed character and weak will. This miscalculation has cost many the victory. Failure to understand the spiritual nature of the conflict will bring sure defeat in a battlefield where even our own thoughts and feelings cannot be trusted.

In his struggle to deceive and overcome us, the Enemy has tampered with everything, including our own perceptions of who we are. Our souls have been caught in an internal ambush. The Devil has set us up to be the enemy we fight by pressuring us into believing the lies we hear ourselves telling ourselves. He does this by impersonating us to ourselves in ways that make us think we're thinking that thought ourselves. He has not only blocked the path of truth but has hidden snipers along the well-traveled roads of recovery in order to shoot at us.

The *Deceiver* provokes a crisis by taking advantage of our human vulnerabilities. He then creates an adverse reaction to that crisis, which then creates a perfect opportunity for *Deception* to come in and offer us a solution to the problem he set up. This Hegelian Dialectic is an old and often-used game plan initiated by the Evil One to pull us into a conflict that ends in the conquest of our own souls. His wiles have rendered us powerless and ineffective in the management of our own lives, the kingdom of self we individually identify and call by our own names.

Every attempt we make to take back our lives on our own gives the Enemy another insidious opportunity to intensify his grip on us and establish his stronghold in us until he has secure complete control of us. Human pain creates desperation. *Desperation* becomes a great motivator. *Panic* marches on in an endless parade of external and immediate "self-help" remedies and snake-oil medicines that mint a fortune. The Devil reaps huge benefits on either side of the conflict at the expense of the afflicted.

In every place we appear motivated to do something the Enemy rallies to take the opportunity he created to assist us. Whether it is our desire to lose weight or to overcome an addiction or heal a relationship, he and his world system have a plan. The diets and the "do more" recommendations of those touted to be the experts in the area of discipline have given us an endless number of ways to enhance our sex lives, lose weight, and quit using while others sell us their indulgent diet plan that permits us to eat the sugar-laced delicacies of the privileged without gaining a pound. So, which is it?

The Enemy even uses our desire to know God and be good as bait in our common human quest for happiness and security. For centuries the Tempter has used our feelings as major motivators in getting us to go along with his suggestions. We become wrapped up in looking for pleasure as defined by success, as defined by security, and as defined by having enough money which becomes the bottom line on having a wonderful life. It is all up to you. Less fat, more money, less work, more play, less pressure, more things; you can have it all if you just want it bad enough and work harder.

Trying to avoid the consequences of indulgence have sold millions of tabloids and TV ads, not to mention memberships in special weight-reduction clubs where we can purchase special low-calorie, high-calorie, low-carb, high-carb, high-caffeine and caffeine-free foods and fads and exercise gadgets and, and, and … until the only sensible thing left to do is to *stop*!

But wanting more and having all we want have ultimately only left the seekers, the suckers and the "full empty. The pursuit of a beautiful body and the possession of material objects that we have linked with happiness have only filled some of us with a deeper sense of personal discontentment and spiritual void. We've gotten tangled in the "using" trap, trying to fill the emptiness and avoid the pain of life.

Others might still be trying to tell themselves they are happy already, denying they have any problem at all. Still others may try to manipulate the problem to provide for themselves an excuse not to change or a reason to continue to use. We rewrite our standards to redefine the "new normal" as acceptable. What was not acceptable is now the acceptable, new "truth" for judging our health, our world, and ourselves.

We swing back and forth between denying the problem and becoming obsessed with trying to overcome it. We spare no expense to defeat, once and for all, the things that control us, only to fall in the throes of the struggle to stay free. All of this striving leads to more restlessness and dissatisfaction. Ultimately, it morphs into the big distraction of making my life all about me and getting rid of my "sin" or anything else I don't like about me!

Deep inside, we know that our lives are to be all about Him, yet, how many of us have made an excuse or turned a deaf ear to the still, small voice of the Holy Spirit, thinking, "I will but not just yet"? First "I've got to finish losing this weight or get through school or get that promotion or settle down or wait until the kids graduate or ..." It all sounds a lot like the excuses that those invited to the banquet used in turning down the king's invitation to his son's wedding (Lu. 14:15–20).

Freedom from God's Point of View

Nothing has escaped the evil eye of our opponent. For many of us, even our table has become a snare (Ro. 11:7–9). Eating food is a much more spiritual act than most would have suspected. It offers ample opportunities for us to make decisions and be tricked into making the wrong choices on a daily basis. Because not eating is not an option, all of us are subject to the pressures of the Evil One who would lead us to make food a god, a comfort, a recreational pastime, or a distraction. The need to eat has become a place of great vulnerability and a splendid opportunity for the Enemy to implement his takeover to control us.

Cravings makes a case for surrender and deliverance. It addresses our need for freedom from God's point of view and offers real solutions to addiction whether those addictions are in regard to food, substances, behaviors, or relationships. Each of the chapters covers a different aspect of, not only the rules of eating and obeying, but also the power of the internal programming that controls many of the things we are caught doing that we do not want to do.

The Bible describes temptation as something "common to man" (1 Cor. 10:13). Paul offers us great insight and hope into the demonic activity that operates behind it and admonishes us saying "Let not sin therefore rule as king in your mortal (short-lived, perishable) bodies, to make you yield to its cravings, and be subject to its lusts and evil passions." (Ro. 6:12, AMP). James outlines the matter of temptation as the act of one being "drawn away by his own desires and enticed" (Ja. 1:14).

Cravings helps the reader link the two. When temptation and desire come together, sin is conceived. Only in understanding the truth about spiritual warfare and the finished work of Christ on Calvary do we gain the revelation necessary to walk in the freedom He died to give us. The true and simple essence of the Gospel is one of grace. His Gospel is not one of "do" or "do more" but "done"!

The second half of the book outlines the scientific operations and functions under which the "fearfully and wonderfully made" (Ps. 139:14) human body makes its responses to cravings. Understand how frequencies, the nervous system, and the basic human need for food and nutrition make us vulnerable to the pressures of both the physical and spiritual worlds give us the first steps to freedom. Realizing our human bodies have been bound by certain natural constraints and biological functions makes the questions of willpower and victory even more elusive and the answers more compelling.

Chapter 1

Eat What I Give You

C raving is defined as a strong desire to have something—to demand or to force, through devious means. The power of the lie behind cravings began when the Serpent's dialogue with Eve aroused her curiosity to know what was on the Forbidden Tree. How could something so forbidden be so bad when it looked so beautiful? Hoping she would want to know more than she already did, the Enemy used her desire to know more, which, indeed, worked like a charm.

Humanly speaking, we are often pulled more deeply into a situation in our very wish to avoid it. The same is true with the desire to satisfy an urge. We get caught between the desire to satisfy a craving and the need to resist it. We are torn between self-indulgence and self-control and often spend ourselves trying to quit doing something we cannot seem to stop. The paradox that locks us in a vicious circle of failure and addiction is as maddening as it is debilitating.

God planted a garden, eastward in Eden. There He put the man whom He had formed. (Gen. 2:8). Life was simple and the setting serene. No concrete jungles or pressing deadlines or sickness filled this paradise. The Lord God had set up an environment with the perfect conditions for the care and keeping of the man and his body. Out of the man He created woman. Every element they would need, including the food required to keep their bodies healthy and beautiful had been given to them as the herbs of the field and the fruit that grew on the trees of the garden.

The preservation of life and the health of their bodies were of great importance. God, therefore, prioritized His instructions to them about what they should eat. Food preparation would be as simple as picking and eating. Everything was raw. Kitchens and cookbooks were unnecessary. Eating would be as instant and enjoyable as breathing was effortless.

The command given to Adam and Eve to eat the fruit and the green herb is the very same command God has given to us, passed down through the same Word He gave them. He did not intend to limit our freedom or control our eating habits. He simply wanted to protect us. God was not trying to stifle us or infringe upon our free will any more than the manufacturer of our car is trying to restrict our use of the car by issuing certain warnings and maintenance procedures. These recommendations are made to enhance the life and performance of the vehicle as well as protect the owner, not to control him.

As a matter of fact, most of us take the manufacturer's guide in caring for our cars and lawn mowers more seriously than those given to us by God in caring for our own bodies. Even if we chose to disregard his advice, we are not be offended with the manufacturer or accuse him of "messing" with our free will or charge him with not knowing what he was talking about.

Such is often not the case with the Creator of heaven and earth. Many of us choose to disregard His Words, if indeed, we acknowledge them at all. Some of us take the gift of life and the body He gave us for granted to the point of self-destruction. We drive them into the ground literally, through ignorance, neglect, or intentional abuse. Others indulge their appetites by making their belly their god and their bodies the instrument of self-gratification.

The trouble is, many of us do not realize how "fearfully and wonderfully" we have been made or how serious this "eating thing" really is until something goes wrong and it is too late. For the wise, the severity of the matter strikes us when we finally realize, personally, that "this is the only body I will get. It is the same body I will have to live in every day for the rest of my earthly life."

But even in our ignorance, God has built in protections in anticipation of those things that would target the body to destroy it. He has given us an amazing immune system to defend us and disarm invaders. The body has been equipped with detoxification and purifying systems to regenerate and renew every cell. Its memory capabilities are incredible and its communication systems keep the body well connected and its members well informed. When all parts work together in harmony and equity, the strength and health of the body are preserved and life is good.

The body not only provides us with the house we live in but becomes the place where our lives are sustained through the trillions of chemical functions and interactions done every day without even our conscious awareness. And, as it is the sacred place of human habitation where each of us live, it is also the battlefield where the greatest conflicts between God and Satan are fought.

Through the marvelous working of its parts when given the proper nutrients and essential elements it needs, the body has been given the power to recover and heal itself. Our food is not only an important source of energy necessary to sustain our external activities, it is also vital in maintaining the defense system that protects and shields us from sickness and disease.

God has commanded and created every kind of system and function inside of the human body to address any kind of issue from cell repair to the removal of toxins. He has also designed us with great ability to be able to do work, to adapt to adverse conditions, store fuel, defend ourselves and be in relationship with Him. Truly, our bodies are a testimony to God's great workmanship and His understanding of architectural design even as seen in His anticipation of the many adverse and difficult conditions we would face. For all of this, food is its fuel.

In all fairness, however, we must know there are limits to this miraculous mixture of mud and water beyond which the body will not function well. Those limits begin when lies replace the truth. Neglect and abuse replace love when we disregard eating our food with thanksgiving. Ultimately the body is no longer able to perform its life operations, and we die.

The Original Plan for Man and His Body:

Sickness and disease were not part of the original plan operating in the Garden of God. Obesity and heart disease and addiction to toxic chemicals came as part of the curse. And though God knew the adversity our bodies would become subjected to and the critical part food would play in the maintenance of the body's health, He allowed us a great deal of leeway in choosing and combining those foods. His lavish supply of colors and textures and tastes was generous beyond what necessity needed to make the body strong. God made sure everyone would have lots of good things to eat even if they did not like everything.

So how is it that so many of us have developed aversions and allergies to God's foods? Who would ever have thought we would find so many ways to adulterate the food and spin the molecules and counterfeit taste and process the textures to adapt the food more to our liking? And who would have thought we would make so many excuses complaining about eating the food God made?

And the LORD God took the man and put him in the Garden of Eden to tend and keep it. "And the LORD God commanded the man, saying, 'Of every tree of the garden you may freely eat; but of the tree of the knowledge of good and evil you shall not eat, for in the day that you eat of it you shall surely die.' " (Ge. 2:16–17).

The Second Commandment

The first commandment given to Adam and Eve was to be fruitful and multiply. In the second commandment, God told them what to eat. In the third commandment, He warned them what not to eat. Through God's instructions in the Garden, He made it as clear about what they were to eat as He did about what they were not to eat. They were not to eat of the one tree that grew in the center of the Garden, the Tree of the Knowledge of Good and Evil. Their obedience to this commandment was the hinge-point upon which their very spiritual life and relationship with God depended. The issue was so serious that God warned them that death would be the outcome if they disregarded it.

Two of the first three commandments were connected with food. The first sin was connected with food. The Man and the Woman did what God had told them not to do. They ate of the forbidden fruit. Eating the fruit off of the tree of the Knowledge of Good and Evil was the act of rebellion against God that opened the floodgates of Hell. Evil and destruction filled the Garden, and the souls of the Man and the Woman were taken over by the Tempter.

In that moment, all of earth and its creatures fell under the dominion and control of Satan, and since then, we have become the fuel that supplies his insatiable appetite for lust and blood and power. For all our technology and modern advancements from that moment to this, nothing has really changed, except for one thing. The Cross would be the one thing that changed everything. God Himself redeemed the chapters of war and bloodshed with the incarnation of His Son and the intervention of the Cross. Through Christ Jesus the Father erased the line of transgression that separated us from Him by inviting "whosoever will" to turn the page on slavery and be written in the Lamb's Book of Life.

Man's Free Will and the Act of Eating

Though none of us have ever eaten of the Forbidden Tree, how many of us have not recklessly eaten strange and forbidden things without giving a thought to the ramifications of our actions? In our disobedience, are we any less guilty than Adam and Eve in bending and breaking the rules of "foods-not-to-be-eaten"—and if, on a regular basis, we have broken the laws of eating ourselves, how do we have any right to fault Eve and Adam for breaking the commandment by eating of the Forbidden Tree?

The question becomes, is our disobedience intentional or the deliberate intention of something that has come to manage our appetites and control our eating? How many of us have been persuaded to eat according to our own personal preferences and undefined cravings? How many of us have been captivated through the seduction of clever marketing campaigns? If the first act of sin and rebellion was committed in regard to eating forbidden food, is it any wonder that food and the capture of the appetite have remained such a strategic battle point in the Enemy's plan for destroying the souls of men? Who would think so great a matter as our relationship with God through Christ could hinge on such a trivial thing as choosing the food we eat? Eating and not eating is not a law used to determine our salvation, some would argue, though it may be critical to our health. Thus, they dismiss the importance of the food we eat as small potatoes, in our walk with God, hardly a study worthy of spiritual discussion.

Satan is astonishingly clever. He has simultaneously pushed the choosing of the foods we eat to the back burner of our minds while secretly making it one of his primary strategies for capture and control in playing his spiritual "hunger games" for our souls. He reprioritizes eating foods that God commanded us to eat as not that important in the determining of spiritual matters.

A closer look, however, might reveal a more hidden danger, if not indeed, a cause for us to at least pause and wonder. Food has always been a reliable weapon in the Devil's master plan for human destruction. If eating the forbidden fruit worked so well in his original takeover of the kingdom, why wouldn't it work again? And, if eating the forbidden fruit had become the point of contention that tipped the scales in the first place, what would make us think eating and choosing our food is any less important today? That leaves us with a real and practical question: how does it all work?

The Danger of Eating Begins before I Open My Mouth

Choosing the food we eat becomes an opportunity to exercise our free will. Any place where we have an opportunity to exercise our free will and make a choice becomes a place where rebellion and disobedience can enter. And because there are specific biological and emotional consequences that come with both eating and disregarding of the laws of eating, choosing the food we eat presents the Enemy with limitless possibilities to deceive and destroy us.

We are God's masterpiece and His crowning glory; the temple He has chosen to dwell in. What better way to insult God than to assault that which represents Him in what matters most to Him? How better to make God a laughing stock than to vandalize His dwelling place among men? In spite of His grace and the body's resilient abilities in regenerating itself, disregard for His instructions on what and how to eat and maintain the health of our bodies has opened the door to a myriad of ways the Enemy can insult God and mar His image in us.

Is This Legalism?

God's laws of eating are not designed to lock us into legalism any more than the Word of God, which is filled with many laws given to govern the conduct of His people, is meant to put more burdens on us. We are not saved or condemned by what we eat. These rules are meant for our protection, not to become another legalistic opportunity for the Enemy to bring us into condemnation for not eating in a certain, prescribed way. That, however, is not how the Enemy sees it. He sees eating as an opportunity to set up guilt and condemnation in the life of the eater.

The fact that food was and continues to be used in various rituals and religious ceremonies also reveals our need to understand the powerful spiritual forces that work behind the scenes, even within the context of personal eating habits. Is it possible that the Enemy is gaining access to our souls by using our eating habits and the foods we choose to consume to bring us into bondage? If the Enemy can use our rebellion, disobedience, and ignorance as his justification to take destructive action against us, then whenever we disregard the commandments of God, even if those commandments were intended by God to be for our protection, we are vulnerable to the accusations and judgments of the Evil One.

In His mercy and grace, God has given us resilient bodies that can repair and recover and rebuild damaged systems. Eating the food God has prescribed for us will optimize our eating to produce vitality and endurance. As in every place where man finds himself free to exercise his free will, choosing what we will eat becomes a place of potential temptation or and disobedience.

God has prepared a safety zone for those who choose to obey His guidelines and eat the green herbs and the fruit with the seed in it. Incorporating these foods and herbs into our diet allow us to take full advantage of the protection His commandment offers to those willing to believe and submit to it. God does not want to make us paranoid or establish eating as another form of religious works or duty. He simply wants to alert us to the dangers of the negative consequences attached to not eating the foods He has given us.

Those who willfully indulge their appetites and disregard the rules of eating open themselves up to sickness and physical depletion of their biological systems. This makes us prone to all manner of dysfunction, including stress, fear, depression, and disease. Eating is meant to be the way we nourish our bodies, given within the context of God's love and provision. Eating God's way becomes an act of obedience. Obedience allows us to eat without guilt and with thanksgiving. If God meant food and the eating of it to be a place of nourishment and blessing to sustain our health and energy, then we can begin to understand why so many are tormented and sick.

Overlooked

It is all too easy to overlook the act of choosing our food as one of Satan's most clever ways to attack and destroy the human body. Even as some may think it not wise to make too much of this matter of eating, it may prove to be just as foolish to make too little of it. Underestimating the power of eating to corrupt the strength of man, or thinking that it would be spiritually off limits in this battle between good and evil only increases its strategic usefulness to the Enemy.

Letting the Man choose what he wanted to eat still presents man with one of his most often used and abused opportunities to exercise his free will every day. Ignorance in not realizing the importance of those choices gave him an unlimited opportunity to participate in his own demise even as he sought to preserve his life. We must examine the possibility of being controlled by cravings, lusts, and evil passions, as well as the need for deliverance from this "body of death" (Ro. 7:24).

"Food for Thought"

Some people determine the level of their sense of safety and worth by the amount and ease of access they have to eating the food they like. Up until now, having food has not been an issue for many of us, but because food is essential to survival, we are all vulnerable to its availability. Those who have the food, as Joseph did in Egypt, have the power. Therefore, whoever controls the food controls us. If that power is evil, those who do not have the food become desperate pawns at the mercy of the one who does. Food, therefore, weighs in heavily on both sides of the equation for power and control.

The lack of it sets us up for starvation, one of *Death's* greatest instruments in harvesting human souls. The abundance of it gives *Gluttony* and *Indulgence* ample opportunity to mock those better positioned at the table and makes it a snare to them (Ro. 11:9–10). Whichever way it goes, too little and too much can both be used to the Enemy's advantage. Obviously, the battle over food is as multifaceted as the possibilities of tampering with it or manipulating its supply are endless.

God meant for food to be a blessing and a sign of His daily presence and provision. How many times has He demonstrated His personal care for the people by providing them with food, manna, for forty years in the wilderness, and feeding the 5,000? He promised He would "not allow the righteous to be forsaken or their seed left begging for bread" (Ps. 37:25). Jesus instructed us to pray, "Give us this day our daily bread," a faith-building exercise most of us hope we never have to use.

- How do you treat your body?
- What are the "gotta have" items on your food list?
- How does your grocery list compare to God's?
- Do you have a covetous relationship with your food?

Chapter 2

Don't Touch My Food

As we tend to own and personalize everything, the idea of "my food" finds its place among the many other things identified on our lists of personal possessions. The idea of owning our food, or wanting certain food, or eating only the foods we like has become commonplace. How many parents have not heard their child say, "I don't like ____"? Picky eating is a common practice especially in the Western World where abundance has been more the norm. (See *Living to Eat or Eating to Live* (two-CD set) at www.liferecovery.com.)

The Enemy internalizes those likes and dislikes and uses them as a reinforcement to influence and control our appetites. Thus, our choices in food are shaped by our taste buds and eating habits. Reinforcement of the pattern and repetition begin to write those preferences into our minds, and the programming is established. "My Food" becomes a subtle motivator that determines what is eaten and what is rejected. Those caught in this snare have come under the unidentified influence of a *feeling* identified as a *craving*. These cravings control the choices as to which foods are rejected, eaten, or overeaten.

Food has also been made into a money-making recreational activity that is no longer used only for nourishment or received as a blessing. It is used for comfort, to fill the emptiness or calm our anxieties. It has become an expression of social status, personal rights, and economic security. The Bible warns that those controlled by their stomachs are subject to becoming "enemies of the cross of Christ: whose end is destruction, whose god is their belly, and whose glory is in their shame—who set their mind on earthly things." (Phil. 3:18–19).

Eating by the Rules

It may sound like over spiritualizing to make eating good food an act of obedience, but that is exactly what God did. If God gave a commandment, then breaking that commandment is possible, just like posting a speed limit now makes speeding a violation of the law. Before the posting, you could drive as fast as you wanted without fear of being stopped for speeding and given a ticket.

Under the strictest interpretation of the Law, the curse matches the offense. The biblical precedent for this is clearly seen in the well-known passages, "an eye for an eye" and "a tooth for a tooth," (Ex. 21:24). Notice how the curses that God pronounces upon Adam and Eve for eating the forbidden fruit all relate directly to the gathering and production of food. The ground became cursed. The food would be gathered in the sweat of their brow. The ground would produce thorns and thistles. To this very day, the effects of this curse remain, bearing witness to the continued presence of the curse itself.

Isn't it comforting to know (I'm being sarcastic here) that whenever God enforces a consequence, the Devil can play it either way. He can shake his finger at us and make us feel guilty and deserving of the bad things that come out of God's chastening or He can come to our aid and act like our "savior" to "deliver us" from the wrath of an all-powerful but "mean" God who is being unfair in letting all these bad things happen to us in the first place.

The Devil has no problem shaking his finger at God and often does just that in providing us with his own dia-bolical recompense for sin or by offering us a temporary distraction or false comfort to hinder us in coming to true repentance. Alas, the Enemy's solutions to deliver us from the "cruelty of God" are only a temporary fix to keep us from knowing the truth. The discipline of God is intended to bring us to repentance and restoration, not reduce us to the ash heap.

Taking the Devil's shortcut solutions to a "better life" only increase and intensify the problems the Enemy claims those quick fixes would have cured. Take deodorant, man's answer to sweat, for example. Most of the popular brands are filled with aluminum, a known cancer-producing agent. How many bodies have died by succumbing to the deadly effects of sweat in comparison to those who have died from lymph cancer due to the use of antiperspirants laced with aluminum zirconium, for fear of offending someone? As if there are no natural deodorizers that God has given us to deal with sweat!

What about the various chemical fertilizers and GMOs (Genetically Modified Organisms) that have been created to increase yields that have only produced curiously-altered food and put more pressure on our bodies to detoxify substances they do not recognize. As it turns out, the sweat and the weeds are far less lethal than the Devil's solution to deal with either of them. As a matter of fact, many of the weeds are now being rediscovered as actual remedies that carry the cures for a countless number of physical ailments laid down by the curses!

So why did God make a law if He knew people would just break it? For the same basic reason we pass laws in society: to keep people from getting killed, ripped off, and treated unfairly. We must understand that the law does not bring with it the power to make anyone keep it, in spite of the consequences. We still have the freedom to ignore or disregard the protection it affords. There is no incentive to keep the law as a means of justification since keeping the law cannot justify us.

In other words, keeping the law does not make us righteous because keeping the law or making more laws is not the remedy for sin. The curse of sin was death. No amount of obedience, after the fact, could change that. The only remedy for sin, which caused death, was death. That death could only be given by one who was qualified to die, not one already slated to die under the curse. Only the One who came from outside the system of earth would be qualified to give His life. Only the One who came down from heaven was eligible to die. And that is exactly what He did. (Jn. 6:41–51).

The "sting of death is sin and the strength of sin is the law." (1 Cor. 15:56). What begins as a little sting of sin ends up as full-blown Death. The sting of sin gets its lethal power from the law. Death is the final destination for disobedience. God loved us enough to make the supreme sacrifice to die in our place. He ransomed us knowing He would be misunderstood and held in contempt for it. For that reason Jesus Christ is the most loved and hated of all human beings who ever drew the breath of life. Dying in our place is love's beginning point.

Obeying God's command to eat the food He has prescribed for us brings us into covenant with God's grace and protection. It makes the consequences of our obedience to eat the food He gave us almost as serious as the commandment God gave Adam and Eve in telling them what *not* to eat. To disobey God's command on what to eat has physical consequences that bring physical death much like spiritual death came as a consequence for eating from the Forbidden Tree.

Just because God did not personally pull us aside and instruct us on the benefits of obeying the laws He set up for eating does not exempt us from the consequences for ignoring them. Not seeing the immediate effects of violating those laws has led many to eat without considering the long-term damage that comes from disregarding them. Because eating is vital to human health and functioning and because we must make numerous choices every day about what we will eat, eating gives the Enemy countless opportunities to tempt and deceive us.

Ezekiel 2:6–8 makes a striking connection between rebellion and eating. God speaking to Ezekiel says, "Do not be afraid or dismayed. Though they are a rebellious house … speak My words to them, But you, son of man, hear what I say to you … Do not be rebellious like that rebellious house; *open your mouth and eat what I give you*" (emphasis added).

From this passage we can see that eating what God gives us becomes an indication of our submission to Him, an act of obedience and a source of blessing. Not heeding His provision and command becomes a sin that brings a curse upon the land and opens the door to death (See Pr. 26:2). The law of sin and death was authorized under the declaration that "the soul that sins shall die" (Ez. 18:4). Sin, in turn, activated the "body of death operating software" that was downloaded into Adam and Eve when they ate the fruit of the Forbidden Tree. The body of death has become a permanent part of the programming that controls the human functioning of the unregenerate soul. It contains all the operating instructions and accumulated agreements of the generations past that permit the Enemy full access to our body and soul.

In agreeing with the counsel of the Serpent, Adam and Eve acted on the lie and chose to partake of the forbidden fruit. This yielded up the souls and bodies of our first parents to death. When the body of death was activated in their flesh, they, and all that pertained to them, became slaves to the spirit of death and destruction. Craving became their master, contracted under an agreement made with "the lust of the flesh, the lust of the eyes, and the pride of life" (1 Jn. 2:16). Their eternal youth and beauty began to fade into aging and decay. Their bodies became subject to sickness, pain, sweat, and fatigue.

Rebellion and the Problem of Blindness

In Ezekiel 12:1–2, God tells Ezekiel he "live(s) in the midst of a rebellious house, having eyes they do not see, and having ears they do not hear." Eyes that do not see the consequences and ears that do not hear instruction create hardening of the heart and spiritual blindness. Through this passage we see the biblical definition of rebellion is "having eyes that do not see, and ears that do not hear and a heart that does not understand" (Ez. 12:1–2). Other scriptures that confirm this picture of rebellion as disregarding instruction and embracing hardness of heart can be found in (Is. 50:4–5), (Is. 6:8–10) and (Ro. 1:18–32). Stubbornness and resistance to God's truth locks the person into a certain state of blindness that makes them unteachable and puts them at risk for more deception.

The most obvious problem with being blind is that one cannot see. Physically blind people have a distinct advantage over those who are spiritually blind in that they *know* they are blind. This gives them clear advantages over those who are spiritually blind but do not know they do not see. The light of their hearts has become darkened, and their hearts have become hardened. If they do not change, they will die in their sins, and yet, how will they be able to see what they cannot see if they cannot see? If they do not realize what they are doing or not doing is creating a problem, how can they realize the need for change? (This is by far one of the bigger challenges in getting people to see the need to change anything, including their lifestyle and eating habits.)

Jesus describes this condition as a false light or deception when He said, "If the light that is in you be darkness, how great and impenetrable is that darkness?" (Mt. 6:23). In light of this impenetrable darkness that covered the eyes of the people, Jesus began His ministry on earth by charging the people to "repent and believe in the gospel" (Mk. 1:15). Put away what you think about things and change your mind. Come into agreement with what God has to say and live.

Paul takes the act of disobedience and disregard for God's plan of salvation even deeper than its effects upon our spiritual life when he links obedience to our relationships with our food to our physical and mental health. In Romans 11 he makes a direct connection between those who refuse grace and those whose table becomes a snare to them. The "spirit of stupor" settles over them, which closes their eyes and ears and causes their backs to bow down.

> What then? Israel has not obtained what it seeks, but the elect have obtained it, and the rest were hardened. Just as it is written: God has given them a spirit of stupor, eyes that they should not see and ears that they should not hear, to this very day. And David says: Let their *table*, (a place of eating and treaty making and relationship building and union and communion), become a snare and a trap, a stumbling block and a recompense to them; let their eyes be darkened, that they may not see, and bow down their back always." (Ro. 11:7–10; emphasis added)

Has our table become a snare to us? Has continuing to embrace *works* or the mixture of *works* and *grace* and the refusal of God's grace created a link to defeat and an opening for depression in our lives? Has the refusal of grace in exchange for the rigidity of a gospel of works and tradition opened the door to a myriad of health problems, including anxiety, fatigue, and stress?

Has our table become a snare to us as a result of our "don't tell me what to do" attitude toward God and His commandments? Are we being deceived and destroyed and consumed by the very things we consume in an effort to sustain ourselves? Has our food become a snare and a trap and a judgment against us because of our rejection and disregard for God's provision, not only for redemption through grace, but nourishment through the foods He has given us?

The trouble with most of us in reading God's word is that we view it through our own personal or political interpretation, reflected in our theological or denominational preferences, and never heed the full implication of God's Word. Could it be that refusing to submit to the grace of the Gospel of God has physical ramifications? Could this be the hardening God warned us about? Has choosing the "works of the law" in practicing religion over the grace of God hardened our hearts and made our table a trap and a snare?

Hardness is not usually a good sign of physical or spiritual health, as we know. Hardening of the arteries, rigidity in the cell walls, stiffening in the joints, and brittle bones all hinder the free exchange of vital nutrients in the body and osmosis in the cells. When we choose to exercise our free will to ignore God's commands in the care and feeding of the soul, the body begins to suffer from the effects of that disobedience.

The body is the vessel designed to carry our soul and our spirit. It is created to respond to the systems that control it. If I eat what I want to eat and drink what I want to drink and no one is going to tell me any different, I am showing complete or partial disregard for the purpose or manner in which God says food is to be eaten. I come into agreement with rebellion, which sets the stage for the internal takeover of my biological systems.

The external attitudes and situations are the outcome of internal decisions which cycle around to affect the health and condition of our bodies at an ever-deepening level of destruction. Disharmony and injustice begin to take their toll inside of us. *Bitterness* begins to burn away at our insides, creating inflammation and arthritis in our joints. To restore health, justice and the free and harmonious exchange of vital elements between cells and organs must be re-established within the body.

Obedience must be restored in our relationship with God, ourselves, and our food before real health and peace will return to our bodies. Isaiah 6:10 makes the connection between rebellion and healing clear: "Make the heart of this people dull and their ears heavy, and shut their eyes; lest they see with their eyes, and hear with their ears, and understand with their heart and return and be healed."

The spirit of stupor and the accompanying blindness come from swapping out works for grace. The spirit of stupor keeps us from seeing the direct and ongoing connection between the first agreement made with rebellion in eating the forbidden fruit and all the physical infirmities we have suffered from that day to this.

Eating is an expression of our freedom of choice, making it something the Enemy can contaminate and influence and control quite easily. Because food is vital to life and the proper function of its delicate systems, how would the Enemy not consider it one of his most promising and effective tools in destroying us?

Who would have ever thought we would get into food fights with the Devil? Using food as a weapon in the war he is waging against the Kingdom of God seems unbelievable until we realize the critical part food plays in the life of the body. (See *Eating for Spiritual Health* (two-CD set) www.liferecovery.com.)

Just How "Picky" Are You?

Maybe it is time to check your resistance levels. With all the different colors and sizes and shapes and textures and variety of foods that God has created, juicy and tart and solid and sweet and mild and hot, fresh, dried, and freely given, it seems hard to imagine there could be so much "fussing" over food. You would think we could all find at least a few things "made without hands" that would appeal to even the pickiest eaters among us.

The food we eat also has a lot to do with how we feel about ourselves and the energy we need to live. Our physical appearance and body image become a powerful determiner of our sense of worth and instrumental in defining the level of personal happiness and satisfaction we feel about ourselves. Because food is so tied into our weight and energy levels, it becomes a critical factor in both our self-concepts and our health. What better, simpler way for the Enemy to control and change the quality and direction of our lives than to control us through the food we eat?

Beware of Deadly Delicacies

Some foods are not only harmful but also deceptive as is well supported in scripture. Proverbs says, "Put a knife to your throat if you are a man given to appetite. Do not desire the king's delicacies, for they are deceptive food." (Pr. 23: 2–3).

Could the scripture's warning of the deceptive powers of the king's delicacies collaborate with the scientific findings about the detrimental correlation between sugar and refined flour and their effects upon the human disposition and brain functioning? What about the even more deadly additives made to enhance the taste and presentation and preservation of our foods, including MSG and artificial food coloring and flavorings? Do not forget to mention all the other calorie-free fluff and calorie-laden stuff we eat called "junk" food or "fast" food.

- What are some of the foods/substances you eat impulsively?
- How do comfort and the need for safety affect your choice of foods, beverages, and chemical substances?
- Can you name some shortcut food solutions (fast foods, etc.) that have negatively affected your health?
- Has food replaced grace and confidence in the goodness of God with instant gratification, control, and "feel good" feelings?

Chapter 3

The War Within

To better understand the traps *cravings* and *addictions* have set for us, we must take a closer look at how the Enemy operates in our bodies. If we agree that spiritual warfare can exist and operate at every level of human experience, then examining our physical addictions to food and drink from a spiritual perspective is not over-spiritualizing. Many are held in bondage to behaviors they hate. Their true identity and free will are tangled up in the fight with an enemy they believe to be themselves. Not understanding what the Bible has to say has left them stranded somewhere between sin and sickness, with shame and regret as their constant companions.

Our Enemy is wily. Treachery is his specialty. One of his most successful strategies against us is to keep his activity so concealed under the radar that we do not even consider there is a spiritual force manipulating our actions at all. Many of us as do not think of eating as anything more than part of our ordinary everyday life, surely inconsequential in terms of spiritual importance and totally a matter of personal preferences.

Because many of us do not think there could be any spiritual ramifications to the decisions we make regarding the food we eat, we eat in blissful ignorance. Our explanations for the food we eat take us no deeper than taste and appearance. Never suspecting this to be an area where the Enemy would or could set up his intentional plot to ensnare and destroy us, we just eat the food we eat because we like it or it tastes good. Nothing could be further from the truth and more foolish!

As surely as the Devil is real, so are his plans to kill, steal, and destroy us. What better way to do that than to take something we must do several times every day, something which must involve our choosing, and lace it with a lie? Poisoning works especially well when concealed in the intended victim's food or drink.

It is time to wake up. We must stop living in "la-la-land" when it comes to what the Enemy is doing and his intentions to destroy us. In every one of the Gospels we find Jesus dealing with the Devil. The Bible constantly refers to and confirms the theme of spiritual warfare and Satan's activities on the earth, in and among us. References to the activity of demons and the Devil are made in all of the Gospels, the book of Acts, and in almost every Epistle of the New Testament. The oppression of the Enemy was so real that Jesus gave His disciples special authority and protection against the Enemy and specific power to cast out demons (See Lu. 10:1, 19).

Though Satan's tactics to obscure his activity and scare us into not confronting him may have worked well in the past, we do not need to live any longer under his intimidation. God is real. The Devil is real. The war is real. God says not to fear, "I will be with you always, even to the end of the age" (Mt. 28:20). God does not lie. God wants us to know the truth and understand the anatomy of the lie, lest we die. (See *Preparing for Battle* (two-CD set) www.liferecovery.com.)

Because we are made up of body, soul, and spirit, the solution to whatever ails us must address all three levels of our being and functioning. If our answers do not include the needs of every part, our recovery will be only partial and temporary. Often, however, the problem does not get our attention until it surfaces as a physical issue. Though the situation may manifest as pain, the roots lie deeper, hidden in the realm of our soul. Until the roots are dealt with, the troubles in the tree will continue to persist.

The lie is the root. The sin is the fruit, whether it be a sin, a bad habit, or an addiction. Sin is the outgrowth of the lie. A lie cannot be removed by surface measures. Working harder and trying to quit or taking control are all exercises in frustration, futility, and failure. They breed condemnation and discouragement. What is advocated here is not like any of the typical self-help treatment plans or dieting programs you may have tried in the past.

Many of our diet plans and treatment programs omit the notion of a spiritual struggle altogether, while others incorporates it in a way that puts the blame for failure back on the one seeking help, thus deeming the system or program faultless. We are made responsible for the outcome of the program, and if we fail, it is our fault much like failing to get good grades is explained in terms of poor students instead of poor learning environments, trouble at home, or an overburdened educational system.

We are not here to discuss the flaws or merits of our educational systems, but we can agree that there are many more reasons a student can fail than just putting all the blame and responsibility back on the student. The same is true of treatment programs and self-help groups. We have become a self-help society that feeds on striving and still stresses over the insidious cycle of failure and recidivism. Something is not working.

Though wanting freedom is essential to initiating the process, it is, in and of itself, not enough to secure that freedom. The legalistic, religious structure of many treatment programs and self-help methods touted as helpful in recovery only succeed in pushing our already-exhausted systems to a higher level of demand and performance. We are maxed out while the increased confusion makes us feel even more useless and dysfunctional.

Cravings, addictions, and the attempt to control or curb them can only be truly understood when examined from a biblical point of view. To gain real and lasting victory we must let go of our theories and opinions. Even our own experiences can be misleading. What works for one, in the laws of both science and God, should work for another, all other things being equal. But all things are not equal, and nothing works like that.

Though it is true that life happens to all of us, going through similar circumstances does not guarantee the things we believe to be true and real coming out of those experiences are going to be the same for any of us. The uniqueness of our personal experiences and perceptions can create as many different individual responses and reactions to life as there are individuals.

Stuck in a Rut

Trying to get rid of pain and being good are two of the most compelling forces that motivate us to do anything. Though losing weight, staying sober, being happy, sleeping well, and getting our health back are subsequent to these; they all seem to be interconnected with each other. The shame of failure and re-posturing ourselves over and over to get it right, so we can capture the elusive goal freedom has set before us, can quickly turn to defeat and despair.

As eager and desperate as we often are to try new things to alleviate our condition, it is just as amazing to see how fiercely we cling to our old ideas and opinions about how to fix it. Our beliefs rule our thinking and determine our behavior. This closed-minded approach to eating and addictions cuts us off from considering anything different than what we have already considered and locks us into doing the same old thing over and over, expecting new results. Some have defined that as insanity.

Effort is not everything! Without divine help and deliverance, victory in our pursuit of God or His goodness is impossible. Peace with ourselves begins with peace with God. Peace with Him comes when we are in compliance with His commandments. Many of us are willing to settle for the "back side" of true peace, that is, feeling less anxious and emotionally out of control, without getting to the real root of the problem that keeps us from knowing true internal peace.

Defining Cravings as a Spirit of Control

Control is defined as:
- To operate a machine as through the use of programming
- To restrain or limit
- To manage, exercise power or have authority over something or someone
- Ability to run something, operating switch
- To supervise and monitor operations
- Special computer key
- Evil spirits that guide séances to help the medium gain access to the dead

Cravings is often simply described as a strong desire, to want, to demand or beg. It seems the word comes from an old German root for the word craft. Craft is the art of manipulation that forces something or someone to conform to the hand or will of the crafter. The *spirit of Control* works with a *spirit of Cravings* to manipulate its victim into doing certain things through force and under the pressure of intimidation. Witchcraft attempts to manipulate or craft (shape) the minds and actions of its targets by calling upon demonic powers to enforce the spells made over them to change their wills, minds, or circumstances. The word witchcraft comes from the Greek word *pharmacia* from which we get words like pharmacist, pharmacy, and pharmacology. We are all familiar with the mixing and making of medicines prescribed to modify, alter, or manipulate our feelings, thoughts, or the physical symptoms in our body to make us feel better or more normal.

The words *cravings* and *craft* also imply mischievous or devious manipulation, as one skilled in trickery or deceiving others. It would appear that behind cravings is a spiritual force with an agenda of its own. That agenda works to deceive or manipulate the host system to bring it under the control of an evil spirit. That is, in fact, exactly what *Craving spirits* do. They manipulate our internal God-given systems to cause them to dysfunction in such a way as to bring us into bondage.

The *spirit of Cravings,* for example, uses our God-given hunger-satiation system that was given to monitor and manage the intake of food in an orderly and helpful way, to run its own agenda. It bypasses the God-given mandate by rewriting some of the operating code. "Food = nutrition," is the equation as written by God. The Enemy may rewrite it as, "food = comfort." Though food does comfort us by taking away hunger pangs, the Enemy uses those good feelings to condition us to believe food is the remedy for other discomforts such as pain, loneness, anxiety, or frustration.

Those who have been rewired by *Cravings* now believe they need to have certain sweets, carbs, or other "comfort foods" to deal with loneliness or manage their emotional pain. They become dependent on alcohol or drugs in order to feel good. They become distracted by *Obsession,* driven by its obsession to "get stoned" or fix an uncomfortable situation. Often the desire to have these things causes a detrimental alteration in their mood or behavior, which causes them to change their current plans or priorities in relationships, in order to accommodate getting what they think they "gotta have" to survive. They eat or drink or ingest certain things to the point where the negative pressure is somewhat eased. The behavior is turning into an addiction as they begin to come into agreement with the idea that "Using makes me feel better; therefore I will use."

Doing the Thing I Don't Want to Do

Applying the definitions of *cravings* and *control* to our topic will help us see how the presence of underlying forces has come in to manipulate our bodies. How often have we experienced trying to control things we have determined to be undesirable in our lives? We become caught up in a huge outlay of effort and money to stop doing something we hate. But why would I have to stop doing something I do not even want to do in the first place, if indeed, I were not being forced or coerced into doing it? So then—who is really behind what is going on in me, doing the things I hate if it really is not me?

We do not realize the spiritual legalities of the thing we are caught in. It is like trying to back out of a contract we are not even aware of having made. The Devil is a legalist. He will hold us to every detail of that contract until we realize our rights as the blood-bought sons and daughters of God and declare our freedom through confession and repentance. Unless we recognize the power of the passive or subconscious agreement we have made with the lie, and until we cancel out that agreement, the power of the truth to set us free cannot operate consistently in our daily lives.

The Enemy will hold me in the contract of destruction and death. I am stuck, doing the things I hate. I am divided against myself and soon to become my own worst enemy. Trying to stop doing what I am doing makes no sense, unless, of course, it is not me doing it in the first place and I am under the control of another spirit other than my own.

The question becomes what or who is doing in me, the thing I do not want to do? What is acting in me, acting as me and through me, to do the thing I see myself doing that I hate? Paul faced the same discussion and dilemma and concluded it was the *sin* that dwelt *in* him, the one who willed (wanted to) do good (Ro. 7:15–20).

This realization took Paul in a direction few Christians have ever dared to follow. In comparing what Paul says to the way things are taught in the churches today, this biblical declaration sounds like heresy. Arms and eyebrows are raised by those who would proclaim the more sophisticated and finer elements of religion, like taking responsibility and being respectable. They would make victory a matter of willpower, and self-discipline the key to sainthood.

While our intentions and motivation to live a godly life are essential to Christ's command to "follow Me," more willpower and trying harder are *not* the prescription for all of life's sinful woes. Misunderstanding the Gospel of Grace has caused some of those most hungry for God to work the hardest at what they thought was the "will of God" only to find themselves sinking deeper into the pit of exhaustion and depression. They feel condemned for not doing more in the quest to be good enough. Surely this is not the "rest" that is promised to the believer, (Heb. 3:16–4:1) nor is stress a fruit of the Spirit.

- Our main differences are in the things we believe. Knowing that our beliefs have the power to control us, identify your beliefs about food, using chemical substances, and what it looks like to follow God.

- Can you think of any ruts or routines you do over and over again, hoping for a different outcome? Examples might include the way you approach God, how you view yourself, or what it means to take responsibility for your actions.
- Do you use your soul to determine the quality of your spiritual life?
- Do you choose your food to try to manage your emotions?
- Do you think the addiction or other behavior you are trying to overcome will be resolved by more self-discipline?
- Can you think of anything you like about yourself—something you do not think needs changing?
- Can you identify the place where you "surrendered" the food/substance battle to God? How many times have you taken on the task of beating the addiction or trying to get your life back on your own?
- Can you name a few of the insidious demands that take over your mind and capture your will when you are under the influence of alcohol, drugs, or comfort foods?

Chapter 4

Being Redefined by the Devil

To comprehend the full picture of man's condition, we must take a look at it from God's perspective. From God's point of view, man had two problems, which created two problems for God. First, we had been overthrown and enslaved. We had been conquered by the forces of the Kingdom of Darkness. We no longer ruled Eden as free men. Satan now ruled us by subjecting us to do his will.

Second, we had become weakened and corrupted by sin. In other words, the "body of death" or the "body of sin" had infected all the life systems that God had originally set up to serve and protect us. Everything from our immune system to the exercise of our free will had been rewritten to experience death and destruction. Our bodies and our souls had been corrupted with the virus of sin and reprogrammed for an internal takeover.

This double-bind is a very effective strategy for holding one's prey, especially if the captor is not intending to eat his catch immediately and needs the victim to stay alive for some reason. Both are true of our imprisonment by Satan. He still needs us to stay alive and act as a host to provide him with a means to get his needs met. We are meant to be his slaves. Our bodies give his demons a vessel from which they can enjoy their brief reign on earth to the fullest, including satisfying their hideous desires and insatiable lusts, cravings, and vile passions.

God's solution to man's dilemma must also be two-fold. Death (Romans 6) became His solution for extricating us from the Kingdom of Darkness and our unlawful detainment in the prison camps of Hell-on-Earth that operated through the body of sin. Deliverance (Romans 7) became God's solution for removing Satan's internal programming that controlled us through the "body of death operating software."

Just as natural death releases us from the control of this natural world's kingdoms, our spiritual death accomplished vicariously through Christ's death releases us from the control of the Kingdom of Darkness. Through Christ, we are able to reckon the old man dead. Our death in Christ allows God to pluck us out of the Devil's kingdom and transfer our citizenship into the kingdom of His Dear Son (Col. 1:13–14).

Once we are "dead" (symbolically demonstrated through our willing participation in water baptism), we no longer belong to the Kingdom of Darkness. Our citizenship is now in heaven. Death releases us from the Devil's kingdom and makes us eligible to walk in freedom and deliverance. Deliverance is God's solution to the demonic programming that began to operate inside of us, our minds, our emotions, and our bodies at the Fall in Eden.

Am I Bad?

At this point we must make a serious determination not to drift away or be swept into error. The Bible's wording about sin and its effects upon us are very specific. We are described as "enslaved," not depraved. The Bible never uses the terms "sinful human nature" or "depraved" to describe the innate essence of who we are, though our divine nature is one of the Enemy's key points of debate in challenging our value and validity. Our identity as made in the image of God has been targeted from the beginning. If the Devil can get us to doubt our worth and value by confusing the source of our origin through evolution, or call our original nature into question through doctrines that teach the "depravity of man" or its opposite—that man can be as god—he has struck us at the very core of our being.

How does he do this? He simply blurs the distinction between our *being* and our *behavior*. He convinces us that we are acting badly and that we do sinful things because we were born depraved. We have no way, based on the empirical evidence of our sinning, which the Enemy offers as proof of our sinful human nature, to refute the charges, so we make a passive agreement with what seems to be the case, based upon our observation. *I must be bad because I am sinning. I am sinning therefore, I must be bad.* When the facts are reexamined under the counsel of the truth and the fact that he was the one who tempted us for the express purpose of deceiving us into exercising our free will to sin in the first place, his arguments fall apart.

The facts remain that we are born into a blighted and sinful world ruled by the Evil One, a biblical truth and a spiritual fact as given to us by God! Throwing a newborn into a mud puddle or assigning him to difficult circumstances does not make the baby less valuable or prove he is innately depraved or stupid, though the infant will surely become muddy. The child is at the mercy of his or her circumstances, including the possibility of being confused about its own worth and being thrown out with the bathwater which proves it is bad. For clarification purposes, we must remember that God did not create the Pit. He created Paradise.

Using the Pit to reinforce his point, the Enemy has an easy time making his case for our wicked and sinful nature. All he has to do is get us to believe that we are what the experiences of the pit tell us we are. (Obviously, not knowing the Evil One would use every means to get us to agree with the lie, including manipulating and instigating the experiences of the pit to get us to agree we are bad, is to our severe disadvantage).

By very virtue of being born into any pit, however, there is no doubt that the child will get dirty. Are babies washable or must they be thrown out if they get soiled? Do we disown them once they get dirty? Do we define or value our children based on how clean their clothes are? God made us washable both in the natural and cleansed us through the washing of the water of His Word in the spiritual (Eph. 5:26). He has also promised to give His children robes of righteousness. Both the external and internal concerns of sin have already been taken care of.

But what if the child believes the lies of the pit and in its heart believes it is permanently defiled, spoiled, or ruined? For those stains to be removed, we must have a "change of heart." Repentance is changing our mind and heart to believe the truth. It replaces our agreement with the lies (even though they have become more familiar and strangely comfortable) than God's truth. God cannot remove those stains without our cooperation. We must agree with the truth, believing and trusting in Him and His goodness to help us and not hurt us.

The Bible makes a clear distinction between being and behavior. It interprets and describes our behavior as unrighteousness. "There is none righteous, no, not one; ... there is none who does good, no not one" (See Ro. 3:10–18). No one is righteous or is able in their own strength to conduct themselves righteously. Does that mean they are bad and depraved, or could it be that they live in a snake pit and the Serpent is still biting them?

The Bible has always made a distinction between God's righteousness and our self-deceptive attempts to establish our own righteousness. Man's desire to obtain his own righteousness through works apart from God and God's valuation of our worth through His grace form the basis of the main conflict between man and God. If God would accept our good works as the basis for salvation, He would have to disqualify the merit of His Son's shed Blood as the means to Eternal Life.

Second, if God would consider only those who behaved well to be worthy of love, then His love would be conditional. Love correctly defined is unconditional. God's unconditional love made Him open and vulnerable to getting used and abused. Though some have abused His love and grace, using His mercy as "loop hole" to continue in or justify their sin, His gracious goodness continues to be "kind to the unthankful and evil" (Lu. 6:35). His grace neither gives us the right to sin or a reason to reject the Gospel of Grace for fear of sinning. It appears that some of us are willing to tax the limits of His grace to test His patience while others barely believe He gives it at all.

As far as God taking a risk in letting Himself be taken advantage of by us, it appears He was willing to do so to get back the one thing He had lost and couldn't live without—us! Works without grace do not work. Mixing works with grace brings a snare (Ro. 11:5–10). Just as faith without works is dead, so rejection of God's grace is the rejection of God's love. Works are the demonstration of our faith in response to God's grace as we respond to God's invitation to "whosoever will."

The Critical Premise

We are made in the image of God. This is a critical premise from which to begin our understanding of the scriptures. The plan of redemption is one of rescue and recovery through repentance (changing our mind, i.e., stop believing the lie). It is not based on remodeling our character or improving our behavior or self-stylizing our divinity. In the discussion of "who I am," it is essential that we continue to maintain the distinctions between *being* and *behavior* because Satan uses our behavior as the basis for his argument to convince us we are bad.

He uses the things I see myself doing to persuade me to believe that I am defined by what I do. If I am what I do, he can trick me into doing things I feel guilty about and hate. If he can get me to agree that doing equals being, he can convince me I am the thing I hate. If I am the thing I hate, then, to get rid of the thing I hate, I must get rid of myself. If I hate the things I am doing, then his solution to this bad behavior is for me to get rid of the things I hate by getting rid of myself. But, how does my getting rid of myself profit the Kingdom of God?

Satan tempts us to sin, and then uses that sin as evidence to convince us we are bad. Because we were created in the image of God, we are innately motivated to not be okay with being bad. Using our innate motivation to prefer goodness, Satan comes into our minds to convince us, through our faults and failures, that we are bad and need to be good.

His reasoning works well to trick us into trading our first nature, which is our divine nature, for our second nature, which we have been taught to call our sinful human nature. He uses the evidence of our sin to convince us we are bad and thus in dire need of one of his standard, tailor-made religious programs to address that sin. In his sinister plot to destroy us, he sets us up in one of his spiritual rehabilitation programs. Then he sends in a "Pious Deceiver" who operates as our guide in his get-it-right, never-enough works program and pretends to be our benefactor in the recovery process. Operating in us as a sponsor in this demonically engineered support system, this self-appointed "spiritual guidance counselor" offers solutions to help us reform and assists us in the process of "getting our act together for God."

Using our divine hatred for sin as the motivation to clean up our lives, he offers us the worldly wisdom of natural solutions that are fueled by our internal desire to be good, get closer to God, and do better. We fall for his suggestions and try harder. Agreeing with the Enemy's suggestions on how to be good, get free, and love God more, we unwittingly give him permission to come in as the "pious deceiver." He sets up his "angel-of-light assistance programs" to frustrate us. If his plot designed to destroy us goes undetected, we are bound in his endless demands, stuck in a recycling of religious performance that is never enough.

Redefined by the Devil

Satan works to redefine who we are by tempting us to take the matters of our righteousness and sanctification into our own hands. He prods us to take responsibility for our behavior. We fall prey to taking his advice on what to do to get better or get rid of a bad habit or get closer to God.

He starts the process by pressing charges against us for bad behavior. He then gets us to accept those charges by agreeing that our behavior is proof that we are bad. This becomes a reason in itself to keep on doing bad things because, if I am bad, I might as well be bad. Bad behavior produces guilt, and is called sin. The Enemy knows how much we hate feeling guilty. Guilt is the viable proof that we were not built to sin in the first place, because if we had been created to sin, we would never feel guilty for sinning. Sinning is contrary to our divine nature. The Enemy uses our feelings of guilt and our hatred of sin as a motivator to get us to "take responsibility" for that sin.

To sin or not to sin becomes the theme of most believers' lives, leaving them far too busy getting their spiritual "act" together to focus on the more urgent matters of making disciples and preaching the Good News. The Good News is that

> Though I walk in the midst of trouble, You will revive me; You will stretch forth Your hand against the wrath of my enemies, and Your right hand will save me. The Lord will perfect that which concerns me; Your mercy and loving-kindness, O Lord, endure forever; forsake not the works of Your own hands. (Ps. 138:7–8, AMP)

The work of our deliverance, which includes both salvation and sanctification, rests upon Him. "There remains therefore a rest for the people of God" (Heb. 4:9). Our work as believers is to labor to enter into His rest by cooperating with the Holy Spirit who has been sent to lead us into all truth. We cooperate and take real responsibility by letting go and allowing God to complete the work He has begun in us, believing that God is faithful to complete the work He has begun in us (Phil. 1:6). As we abide in His Word, He is faithful to finish the work He started in us. Repentance means to change your mind. We let go of the spiritual striving and religious demands and believe what we already know. God is for us, and He is the One who saves us. We turn around and believe that what God says is the truth. (See *Trying to Rest* (two-CD set) www. liferecovery.com.)

Go Back to the Bible

What about our "sinful human nature"? What about the "flesh"? How will God reconcile this apparent resistance to His grace and His call for us to enter into His rest? To answer these questions we must go back to the Bible. In James 1:12–14, it says that each one is tempted when he is drawn away by his own desires and enticed. Our bodies have certain very specific needs, which are formulated as "desires" in us. Those desires and legitimate needs make us especially vulnerable to the pressure of temptation.

If those certain conditions are not met and those necessities are not supplied, our survival is in jeopardy. God created us to need certain things: safety, love, validation, and nutrition, to name a few. We need to be wanted and accepted in order to find meaning and purpose in our lives. There is nothing innately wrong with having needs. Those weaknesses are not necessarily bad, though they do make us more susceptible to considering the quick fix solutions, that come as temptations offered by the Enemy. When those things are not supplied, our sense of well-being decreases. Our anxiety levels go up. We lose our strength and become vulnerable to *Deception* while *Fear* and *Panic* come in, presenting us with the worst-case scenario.

The Bible tells us our flesh is weak, not depraved. Weakness is not sin. Having a need is not wrong. Desiring to fill that need is natural. The outcome can, however, be either bad or good. The Enemy both creates the opportunity and takes advantage of that opportunity to entice us into resolving the problem using his solution rather than the one prescribed by God. We are desperate, in a hurry, and afraid that if we don't do something, things will get worse.

The Devil tempts us to use his remedy to fix our problems, but there are always strings attached when we make a deal with the Devil. We, however, are not immediately aware of those strings, that is, the surrendering our authority and ourselves over to the him, because he dresses the deal up to make it look like it was our idea and we buy into thinking the solution is in taking matters into our own hands. Sin is fixing our problems by doing it on our own.

Being *tempted* by the Devil to sin is *not* sin. Sin comes in when we give into fear and panic and our desires are joined to Hell's solutions. Joining our desires with the Enemy's temptation on how to fix the problem brings forth the conception of sin. The Devil's idea and our agreement unite, like the sperm and the egg. That union brings forth sin. When sin is fully grown, it rises up and kills us (See Ja. 1:12–15). The beginning of sin is separation. If sin is not remedied, sin ends in death.

How Jesus Handled Human Need

Jesus was tempted in the wilderness. He was hungry. The Devil tempted Him to turn stones into bread. What's the sin in that? Which of the commandments forbid the turning of stones into bread? Jesus' hunger was legitimate. So where was the sin in what Satan suggested?

He was enticing Jesus to step ahead of His Father and take matters into His own hands by relying on His own ideas and reasoning. He was challenging Jesus' identity by tempting Jesus to prove who He was by turning stones into bread. If He could do the miracle, He would prove that He was God's Son. How many times are we tempted to prove our worth and establish our identity, that is, "who we are," by doing something in our own strength?

We are afraid to wait so we push ahead to solve the problem or prove our worth or usefulness by pointing to what we did. Jesus knew who He was, and that His distinction as the Son of God was not established by what He did but in who God declared Him to be. Stepping out in a boastful and independent manner would only have got Him to listen to the Devil and surrender all that He was over to Satan. Remember King Saul? (1 Sam. 13:5–14).

How many of our trials are wrapped up in waiting on and trusting in God? The simple answer and summary is: all of them! Waiting for God or waiting on God is a form of dying. We let go and rely on God's direction. We rest and trust in the faithfulness of God when we choose to not run off in our own strength to do something or to get something or try to be something. When we fail to wait, we fail to recognize that the power behind the impatient urgency to act is not God but the Enemy provoking us to take matters into our own hands. Taking matters into our own hands is the first step to becoming *Craving's* prey.

- What happens when you feel pressure to act in your own strength?

Chapter 5

Depraved or Enslaved?

Before there will be freedom from the grip of *Craving's* many forms of addiction, we must get back to the truth about our human worth and the insidious confusion Satan has set up around it. The matter of the sinful nature of man and man's goodness or lack thereof, have been disputed since the church fathers began to talk. How could they account for the terrible things they saw mankind doing without concluding that mankind must be innately evil?

The theory of the depravity of man, like the theory of evolution, is a brilliant, hell-birthed plot to call into question the true identity of both God and man. It has left the door wide open for the Enemy to undermine the goodness of God and completely obscure our own original first nature and holy destiny. In trying to explain the existence of evil and our bad behavior, the Devil has forged a clever lie that denies his existence and swapped out the truth about our divine origin for the idea of a sinful human nature that we are now "hell bent" on fixing.

This conundrum spawned countless debates down through the ages. It seemed self-evident that there was no other way to explain the dreadful things these early theologians saw manifesting in human behavior than to draw the conclusion that man was depraved. Their arguments were based on the observation of man's behavior and the assumption that man is what man does. The idea that man does depraved things; therefore he must be depraved, has created a spiral of circular reasoning that continues to trip up those seeking deliverance and sends all of us chasing our spiritual tails.

"Man does bad things therefore man is depraved and because man is depraved he does bad things" did nothing to clear up the major questions about the plight and purpose of mankind, his need for salvation or the goodness of God. It only raised more speculation and built a larger platform from which guilt and religion could direct the course of the human race. Rather than bridging the gap between man and God and bringing a solution to the immediate problem of man's bad behavior, their explanation complicated matters.

This doctrine of the depravity of man, also known as Calvinism, spread quickly through the ranks of those who sought to understand and explain the things they saw. Their teachings became entrenched in the body of mainline church theology and remains a source of great confusion and division about God and our relationship with Him as our Father to this very day.

Calling for strict adherence to the doctrine of depravity pushed radical Calvinists into a spiritual corner. If man was depraved, he was too bad to even choose salvation for himself. Therefore God had to choose it for him, which then puts God in the very dubious position of selecting who would get saved and go to heaven and who would go to hell. This arbitrary predestination seemed to operate randomly, depending only upon whom God would choose to save. If that were the case, He would be directly responsible for throwing multitudes of people into hell. How does this preselection of only some support God's justice?

The theology of Man's innate depravity makes an assumption that God was forced to have to step in and "sovereignly" save us because we are too bad, (wicked and corrupt) to even desire salvation. Because we cannot or will not choose the gift of salvation for ourselves because we are depraved, God ends up doing all the picking. This forces Him to show partiality and favoritism that cancels out our freedom to choose to accept the Gospel for ourselves.

Further, if God knows everything ahead of time, He knew ahead of time those who He would choose to save. He also knew who would go to Hell. (Some say God is not omniscient and that He does not know everything ahead of time. This doctrine of the non-omniscience of God is another false doctrine that had to be concocted to fix the doctrinal errors of the first wrong doctrine, the depravity of man. By absolving God from the ramifications of knowing all things ahead of time, He was innocent of deliberately creating people for Hell).

If God chose to make all of us, knowing full well some of us would go to Hell because He had not chosen to save them, God would be guilty of the unthinkable crime of deliberately making people He knew beforehand would go to Hell! What kind of a God is that, and who would want to spend time with Him, forever walking on eggshells and living with such a sinister and masochistic Supreme Being?

The elements of God's love and mercy and our free will are all lost in the error of this theology. We are either being forced to go to Heaven or being cast into Hell. (The antithesis of this false doctrine leads to another copious error, that we must be good to prove we are worthy of God's love in order to be saved. Under the influence of this doctrine we are lead to believe God's reward for that good behavior is manifested in getting to go to heaven, when, in fact, we know we are not saved based on how good we are because the Bible says there is none righteous. We are saved by the very act of surrendering to Christ and accepting that we cannot save ourselves, no matter how good we are!)

God does not make anyone to go to Heaven nor does He send anyone to Hell. We have been given a free will. We must choose. If we were not permitted to choose and all was decided by God, as the Calvinists say, God would be as evil an enemy in the destruction of human beings as the Devil is! What God did sovereignly do was predestine all He foreknew to be conformed to the image of His Son. (Ro. 8:29–30). He made the choice to intervene in our lost condition by giving us a chance to choose for ourselves. He came to save "whosoever will" and that is exactly what He did.

Another problem with the theology of the depravity of man is that if only the people God chose to save got into heaven, what is the point of Jesus' death on the Cross or the Great Commission to go and preach the Gospel and make disciples? There is no point! If God has created us depraved, He would be a hypocrite for sending us forth as witnesses to eternal life. We would be like salesmen sent into the region to sell to his prospective buyer a product that does not exist.

The Gospel God gave us would be filled with mixed messages and double standards. He would have contradicted Himself on every tenant of the Kingdom of Heaven to love and forgive one another. He would have insulted His Own Son in making His death on the Cross completely irrelevant and ended up being as unjust and deceptive as the Devil! The theology that endorsed the depravity of man inadvertently must, in its final conclusions, also call God's own character into question.

The depravity of man creates another problem. Logically, if we are created in the image of God according to the Word of God, (Gen. 1:26–27) and God calls Himself the Great I AM THAT I AM, then that would make us "little I am's." If God is Love and loves justice, mercy, and truth, then, He would have had to impart those very same attributes and the desire for them to us. Conversely, if we are depraved and we are made in image of God, then God must also be depraved. (See *Who Am I?* (CD) www. liferecovery.com.)

If, on the other hand, He did not create us depraved but we believe and preach that He did, we are directly linking the depravity of man back to the definition of God. If we had used even the most elementary principles of logic and the basic methods of the scientific research for testing a theory, we would have known how foolish and illogical this idea of the depravity of man is. We would have thrown it out as an erroneous assumption a long time ago. However, instead of admitting our folly, the Devil has continued to persuade us to invest in its merit even to the point of building huge and magnificent structures called churches, which have become a valuable asset in his plundering of souls.

Curiously, all of these observations and conclusions have been developed without putting the Devil into the equation. They make no mention of spiritual warfare or that the Devil is the author of this mayhem. The Devil is a liar and the father of lies (Jn. 8:44). So, why are we so interested in protecting his reputation is beyond reason! Who do we think initiated this question of the depravity of man when the only fruit that comes of it continues to make a case for the depravity of God and the innocence or nonexistence of the Devil?

Why is that? Calvinism omits the obvious by refusing to put the Devil in the equation they use to solve for man's sinful human nature. God already solved the matter of man's enslavement to the Kingdom of Darkness which very clearly explains the observations of man's sinful human nature, with the Cross. The theory of the depravity of man rejects the reality of spiritual warfare including deception and divination that operate as part of the world system.

The Devil as the author of this system affects the mind and heart of every human being to corrupt their behavior by tricking them into fixing their behavior themselves. When they fail, he chides them into believing that it was their sinful human nature and that they just need to try harder to overcome it. What a lie! What a lie they have believed to think it was their choice to fail and sin and separate further from truth in the first place because of their sinful human nature, when it was really the Enemy. He created the concept of our sinful human nature, and then gets us to sin to prove he is right!

The idea of being who God says we are is so obscured that it never even crosses our mind until we hear Paul saying that he "delights in the law of God according to the inward man." (Ro. 7:22). Why would he delight in the law of God if he is depraved or truly defined as innately sinful? The fact that he is struggling, desiring to do the good he wants to do, but cannot because of the sin or evil that dwells in him (Ro. 7:17), proves he was not built to sin. Why would he or any of us really even care if we were good or not if the law of God had not been inscribed on our hearts by the Lord Himself?

The Devil manipulates our lives to set up situations that lead us to choose to do just exactly what fear has led us to choose. We react to that fear precisely how *Fear* and the *Fear of fear* would have us to react. In denying the existence of the Devil, Calvinism fails to factor in the influence of the god of this world with his demonic activity and involvement to corrupt and destroy of us.

The depravity of man is not an adequate explanation for anything including man's immoral behavior. It has, however, left the door open for the nature of man to be defined by his adversary, and has left us defenseless in responding to the charges he presses against us or the case he presents about us before the Court of Heaven. Because we do not know who we are or that he is a manipulator of both the truth and the human behavior, we succumb and plead guilty. How well will we do to believe such a one or be left to the mercy of the one who the Bible calls the Accuser of the Brethren?

All of this theological confusion comes to re-explain what has already been clearly explained in the Scripture. We must put the Devil back in the equation we are using to explain the presence of good and evil in the world before we will get the right answer. Evil and depravity are in the world because the Devil is in the world and he is real. He is evil. He perpetuates sin and destruction; the fruit of his own wicked, heartless behavior among mankind moves forward by deliberate design. His intention is to recreate a race of men in his own image and after his own fallen nature.

The word of God says if we refuse to receive the love of the truth, the Lord will send us a strong delusion that they should believe the lie (2 Thes. 2:10–11). God does not deceive us, but He will (because He must) permit deception to come to those who have rejected the truth. When we refuse to acknowledge that the Devil is real and actively working to destroy us, we are already blinded and walking in the strong delusion to believe a lie.

Though no one likes war, denying the conflict does not make the war any less real or make it go away. Some in the church today are actively enlisted in spiritual warfare, while others prefer to be civilians. Declaring yourself neutral does not protect you. Even civilians can get hurt and become casualties of the war if they do not acknowledge the imminent reality of the danger and move about carelessly in their daily lives.

More Problems with the Theory of Depravity

The Depravity of Man as a theological doctrine makes no sense! It cannot be worked into the equation of Salvation though many, after rewriting the doctrine of salvation, would insist it works just fine! If we would have been born depraved, God would be absolutely unjust to expect us to be good enough to get to heaven by our own deeds, especially since His Word already declared it is impossible for us to establish our own righteousness through good behavior. "There is none good but one and that is God," Jesus said (Lu. 18:18).

But, if God is so good and we are so bad, then how can we ever get to heaven without being perfect? How can we be perfect if we are depraved?" Obviously the gospels of works and futility were both written with the same pen.

The depravity of man is not only contrary to the character of God's love, but it borders on profane ignorance of the Holiness of God. It makes a mockery of the Gospel of Jesus Christ which is the Gospel of Grace.

> But God, who is rich in mercy, because of His great love with which He loved us, even when we were dead in trespasses, made us alive together with Christ.... For by grace you have been saved through faith, and that not of yourselves; it is the gift of God, not of works, lest anyone should boast. For we are His workmanship, created in Christ Jesus for good works, which God prepared beforehand that we should walk in them." (Eph. 2:4–5, 8–10)

The presumptuous tenants of Calvinism twist the Gospel of Grace into "preselection" that gives no hope to those who already see themselves as beyond the hope of God's grace. They conclude that God's salvation is predetermined while others say it must be earned through good works. How confusing is that? Is it grace or is it good works, or is it God just randomly picking who gets in and who does not?

What unbelievable audacity we have embraced to lay our presumptions upon God or His Word. How can we rightly counsel or define God or His Salvation according to our limited and corrupted understanding when Satan has tried to make us part of his own cold-hearted disdain and contempt for God? What absolute hopelessness and confusion this theology has set up in the hearts of any who would seek freedom from a life controlling habit or addiction through works. Nothing works apart from God's grace and salvation.

The Liar would have us believe that Salvation is no longer an invitation to "whosoever will" but rather "whosoever He will." If salvation is only for the chosen few, how could we even imagine trusting or getting justice and forgiveness from the very One Who Himself is suspect of committing crimes even more heinous than those we have seen committed by the demonized among us?

How can those who call themselves Calvinists stand their ground so firmly in the face of such obvious error and not squirm, even a little, at the thought of reducing God to a deeper depth of depravity than they have inadvertently assigned to themselves! What a deliberate perversion of truth! Forged in the fires of Hell to dishearten the souls of mankind, the doctrine of the depravity of man has cut us off from every hope of reconciliation and redemption with God.

A Greater Gulf

For all of us already so painfully separated from Him through sin, the doctrine of the depravity of man does nothing but leave a greater gulf of sorrow and despair fixed between us and our God. It has created more confusion and distrust in the hearts of the unsuspecting and those struggling to be free. It has been successful in separating them even further from the love of God. Deception has twisted the truth and confused them into not knowing what to believe regarding the goodness of God and the continuation of their bad behavior.

God becomes a mysterious mixture of maleficent and merciful. If we are depraved, as the Devil would have us believe, then we are already under the heavy sentence of death. We fall like flies, struck by the blow of Divine wrath as we mindlessly accept the burden of guilt the Devil lays on us. We accept our behavior as full proof of our worthlessness and resign ourselves to fate. Without further consideration or protest, we reject the grace and pardon Jesus Christ died to give us, esteeming it to be a worthless thing!

Alternately, we get mad at God for being so all-powerful and leaving us in such a miserable and helpless state without mercy. How can a good God be so uncaring and ready to cast us off? What kind of a God is that? These questions, left unanswered, have turned many seeking souls away from the Highway of Holiness onto the road of despair and hopelessness. If there is no hope of love or acceptance or freedom for me and God expects me to be perfect before He will have anything to do with me, then I am indeed lost and forever forgotten.

The plan has worked well to bring discouragement and desperation into the hearts of mankind. Raised to believe God is mad at us and can only be satisfied with perfect conduct sets us up to fail the challenge that even the most determined cannot master. Satan has twisted the whole Gospel message of Salvation and Grace into one of works and performance, which essentially boils down to religion, the exact opposite of the truth. Jesus Christ Himself calls us to a Gospel of Grace, to abide and rest our hope fully in His completed work on Calvary. Satan keeps telling us we must earn what God has already freely given!

A veneer slapped on top of a solid oak tabletop could decrease the value of the table to the casual buyer and even cause it to be cast out and destroyed. Only the trained eye of the Master craftsman would see the true value of that which has been obscured by layers of lies and years of futile attempts to repaint the surface. Jesus Christ has come to seek and save that which was "lost," not that which was vile and worthless. Even His story of the widow searching for the lost coin would have made no sense if the coin held no value to her. She was desperate to find it because it was valuable to her! God sees value in us. We are lost. He wants us back!

In Satan's book of lies, the confusion over our origin and identity is both ingenious and indispensable in getting humans to sin and sink into abject hopelessness because of that sin. Satan uses our divine hatred for sin to get us to hate ourselves for sinning while simultaneously getting us to bear full responsibility for that sin. It locks us into the futility of forever trying to obtain that which we are told we can never have. It keeps us from truly knowing that we know we are intimately loved and cared for by the

One who said, "Come unto me all you who labor and are heavy laden, and I will give you rest" (Matt. 11:28–30).

Finally, if God is so unresponsive to our need, how can being with Him for all eternity be much better than being in Hell? In getting man to embrace himself as depraved, the Devil hopes to silence forever every human cry for forgiveness or restoration. The tragedy is that the strength of the Devil's argument is only enhanced by the scriptural ignorance of the Church that promotes it. So the two real questions that remain are: What Gospel have we as the church really been preaching, and what gives us the right to make our own fallible, human explanations about God into Bible doctrines? Ignorance and assumption, perhaps?

Made in the Image of God: The Dispute

Some who endorse the theory of the depravity of man would argue that God created only Adam and Eve in His image and the rest of us were created only in the image of Adam (Gen. 5:3). That presumption brings with it the implication that since the Fall, people were no longer being made in the image of God. If that were the case, why did Eve say at the birth of her son Cain who was born outside of Eden and after the original sin, "I have gotten a man from the LORD" (Gen. 4:1)?

Also, if God had not given her this child, where did Cain come from and who gave him breath, since the Bible clarifies that Cain was Adam's child and not Satan's (Gen. 4:1). Was this an evil child or was this child a child at risk, as were all the rest of the children who would be born from that time to this, who would have to exercise their free will in the midst of constant deception?

Though God had used an unusual method for creating our first parents, shaping Adam out of the dust of the earth and forming Eve using a rib from his side, He chose a new way to generate the rest of us. That method called procreation causes a child to have two natural parents. Newborns commonly bear a natural resemblance to their biological parents. Looking like our natural parents verifies that we are carrying a very specific set of genetic instructions that matches theirs. Those genetic instructions provide us with a distinct set of DNA that forms the foundation of our specific spiritual and biological inheritance. We are both unique in our identity and connected in our ancestry.

Procreation, however, is not a strong enough argument to cancel out or suggest that God is no longer creating human beings in His own image. According to God's own report, He forms us in the matrix of our mother's womb. "By You I have been upheld from my birth; You are He who took me out of my mother's womb." (Ps. 71:6). "For You have formed my inward parts; You have covered me in my mother's womb. I will praise You for I am fearfully and wonderfully made;" (Ps. 139: 13–14). The birth of a child is one of our most sacred "God moments." It is a tangible reminder of the miracle of life and God's presence in it.

Nor does the Adam's image theory tie in well with the various other scriptures that tell us we were known from the foundation of the world (Eph. 1:4; Ro. 8:29–30). The scriptures tell us "Of His own will He brought us forth by the word of truth, that we might be a kind of first fruits of His creatures." (Ja. 1:18).

If God breathed His own breath into Adam and Adam became a living soul, where do the rest of us get our souls from if God is no longer participating in the life-giving process of breathing His breath into us (Gen. 2:7)? And how can any moral obligation or need for salvation be laid on us if our soul is no different from any other animal that lives and breathes? If we are no different, why did God not call the squirrels and whales to repentance? There must be something different about us that God found worth sending His own Son to die in our place.

The Crux of the Problem

Depravity is based on half-truths and used to define *being* by *behavior*. Herein lies the crux of the problem. If the Devil can persuade us to define ourselves by our behavior, all he has to do is question our behavior to raise questions about our divine nature and being. *Self-Doubt* then examines our intentions all the way down to scrutinizing the validity of our salvation. We are confused about who we are because of what we think and how we feel about what God says. The Enemy has gotten us to doubt our desire for God, based on our thoughts and feelings and uses our soul to determine the condition of our spiritual health

The Enemy challenges our divine nature created to resonate with God's love and truth. By agreeing with the evidence of our sin, the Enemy presents his case against us to persuade us we are bad. He then uses our agreement with him and the evidence of our bad behavior to make us second-guess our intentions. *Guilt* comes in to further question our motives, while *Confusion* messes with our identity and questions our origin as being made in the image of God and saved by His grace.

Paul based the revelation of his divine nature upon his agreement with the Law of God. "Now if I do (habitually) what is contrary to my desire, (that means that) I acknowledge and agree that the Law is good (morally excellent) and that I take sides with it" (Ro. 7:16 AMP).

Paul knew that he took sides with the Law. This clarified his motives and intentions, making a strong distinction between him and what he saw himself doing. He saw his delight in the Law of God as a good thing and evidence of his desire for that which was indisputably good. If he knew he desired that which was good, though it was not being reflected in his behavior, he recognized there was something about him that resonated with goodness and truth. He knew that he knew that. That revelation was an epiphany that confirmed to him he was built to resonate with the light of God's truth.

He also knew that there was something dwelling in him that was not good. "For I know that nothing good dwells within me, that is, in my flesh. I can will what is right, but I cannot perform it.—I have the intention and urge to do what is right, but no power to carry it out" (Ro. 7:18 AMP).

The clear distinction between who he was and what he was doing was defined by his will and intentions, not his actions. His being, as defined by his motivation to do what was right, was different and separate from what was going on inside of him. His behavior was being controlled by the "sin which is at home in me and has possession of me" (Ro. 7:17 AMP). That revelation brought him to the realization that he *was not the one* who was doing the deed. (That in itself ought to prompt us to take a fresh look at "taking responsibility" as defined by our theologies and treatment programs and soberly reconsider the true nature of the battle within).

The revelation of our divine nature and who we are from God's point of view is the true premise from which to correctly understand the nature of the two-fold battle we are in, that is, the external one that surrounds us and the internal one that keeps us locked in its strongholds. That revelation is critical in fighting the good fight. The good fight is not a battle to do good things in order to prove we are good. It is not about being good, (which technically implies we are not good) or even about trying to improve ourselves. The command is to resist the Liar who would persuade us that we must prove our worth and earn our salvation through means of our own good behavior in order to please God.

Chapter 6

God Had a Problem

R egarding the discussion of God's problems initiated
in Chapter 4, humanly speaking, we are not the only
ones with a problem here. Romans 6–8 sheds new light
on the two-fold dilemma God faced after our Fall: How
to get back our lives forfeited by our agreement with the
lie and the constant effects of the presence of sin in the
lives of His children.

God's solution to the first problem came in the giving
of His Son to die. Our participation in His death on the
Cross allowed God to substitute Christ's death for our
own. Through that vicarious death and resurrection, we
were disconnected from the demands sin had made on
our life. We were no longer citizens of the Kingdom of
Darkness. Baptism became the symbolic expression of
that death and resurrection. It established a new spiritual
agreement which qualifies us through His resurrection
to be born again and birthed into the Kingdom of God.

The death of Christ fulfills death's demand that the "soul that sins shall die." (Ezek. 18:4). He paid the wages sin had demanded. Through His death we were redeemed (bought back) and translated out of the Kingdom of Darkness and repositioned in the Kingdom of His Dear Son (Col. 1:13). The Prince of Peace has rescued us from the grip of the Prince of Darkness, offering freedom to "whosoever will." Life and freedom were now again made available to those who would choose to believe God.

God's second problem was how to deal with the internal effects of sin and its power to corrupt His children from within. God's solution to the second problem is deliverance. Deliverance is His solution to the internal programming which operates inside of us as the "body of death" (Ro. 7:24). Deliverance and sanctification are opposite sides of the same coin. They both work through our obedience and are sent to dismantle the strongholds of lies the demons use to control us.

Believing the lies of the Enemy has allowed him to reprogram us to sin. Lies have replaced the truth of God's Word. They form the basic structure and commands the Strongman uses to control us. Knowing the truth releases us from the lies and weakens the strongholds where we have been held captive, tormented, and intimidated to do the Devil's will. Some believe this scenario gives too much power and credit to the Enemy and is just an excuse for us to not do something and take responsibility to get rid of our sin.

Paul, however, sees it quite differently. He recognized the severity of the takeover of our souls (the flesh) in his lament when he cried out, "I am sold under sin" (Ro. 7:14). Though it may not at first be apparent, some sort of deal had been made there. Paul realized that sin had made him, along with his first parents and all the generations in between, the purchased possession of the Devil. The evidence of that transaction was in the very sin he found to be residing within him that kept him doing what he hated.

If freedom and the power of the Cross were to be fully implemented, the agreements made with sin would have to be broken at a personal level. Failure to deal with that contract would leave us under the control of Satan. When Christ died on the Cross, He paid the full asking price for our freedom. That freedom was intended to include a full internal recovery of all that was lost as well as the external transfer of citizenship. He whom the Son sets free is free indeed (Jn. 8:36).

However, even after the deal had been done and the work of Calvary was finished, the enforcement of the contracts and the transfer of the titles still are a matter of an individual's decision. Personal choice and free will play an intricate part in determining to what length and how the victory of Calvary will be played out in each individual life. The purchase price has been fully paid. All that was needed to complete the full healing and deliverance of those to be purchased was finished. The deal had been done. The temple property had been bought back by the kingdom of Heaven, so why, then, are we, like Paul, still continuing to experience "Doing the things I do not want to do?" (Ro.7:15).

If Christ has set us free, then sin in any form, including bondage to an addiction or being controlled by cravings, is only evidence that we are still experiencing the body of death, as Paul calls it, operating within us. The presence of that bondage in no way cancels out the full appropriation and effectiveness of the Cross or God's power to save. It merely emphasizes the extreme importance of our willingness to receive the grace of God through the Holy Spirit to appropriate Calvary's victory in our personal life.

We believe what God says in spite of the evil powers that work through the continuing misperceptions and persuasions of our past experiences to enslave us in their lies. King David describes his deliverance this way, "I waited patiently and expectantly for the Lord; and He inclined to me and heard my cry. He drew me up out of a horrible pit [a pit of tumult and destruction], out of the miry clay (froth and slime). And set my feet upon a rock, steadying my steps and establishing my goings." (Ps. 40. 1-2 AMP)

If that be true, then weight loss and the overcoming of a debilitating habit becomes more than a superficial matter solved by willpower and dieting. The struggle to defeat cravings lies buried deep at the core of our spiritual being. Victory and freedom come as we cry out to the LORD for deliverance and understanding.

Must We Stop Sinning to Stay Saved?

God is not unaware of our sin and does not expect us to take care of it ourselves. His Word includes all of us in the sin category by telling us, "All have sinned and fallen short of the glory of God" (Ro. 3:23). The Bible never says humans do not sin or that sinning changes their being (though our behavior, both good and bad, has a powerful effect on our impression of who we are). Scripture does not say we must stop sinning to get saved or stay saved. We must accept Jesus Christ to be saved. The Word of God never presents salvation as a matter of good deeds, or personal worthiness. (See *If I Am Saved Why Do I Still Sin?* (four-CD set) www.liferecovery.com.)

For all of its acknowledgment of human weakness, sinfulness, and disobedience, God's Word never suggests any of these things have the power to strip us of the fact that we are created in the image of God. As much as the Bible makes no connection between man's sin and the rescinding or alteration of his divine origin, it is full of examples of the depravity of man's behavior. Human wickedness is shocking beyond description and is equaled only by examples of its opposite: stories of man's heroism and personal sacrifice.

So if we are depraved, how do we explain the goodness of many, some of whom are not saved yet give of themselves even to the point of suffering and death that others might live? And how does this altruistic, self-sacrificing behavior fit into the theory of the depravity of man? As we see, using behavior as the true test of being only confuses the issue and does not settle the question of our identity or our value for good or for evil.

Freedom Requires That We Understand the Nature of Our Captivity

The Bible offers the only valid solution to the mystery of the conflict between depravity and goodness by describing man as enslaved by sin. "For when you were slaves of sin ..." (Ro. 6:20) makes our first condition clear. "But now since you have been set free from sin ..." (Ro. 6:22) makes our new condition abundantly clear. We were, at one point, slaves to sin. We were part of the plunder the Serpent got at the Battle of the Fall of Man. The rest of the story is about the torment of our captivity and the lengths to which God went to rescue us.

It is hard to see how the theologians could have so missed the point of Romans 6. We were enslaved, not depraved! Though we are capable of doing some very depraved things, depravity and slavery are not the same thing and require two very different solutions. Depravity requires destruction. Slavery calls for liberation.

The problem God faced had become complicated. Satan had captured our bodies. We had been taken over by sin and reconditioned to believe lies more readily than truth. We had yielded our members as the instruments of unrighteousness to sin. Before we were saved, Satan had the right to usurp our human life. We belonged to him, and though it was not fair, it was technically legal. After we get saved, however, we no longer belong to the Devil's kingdom, and anything he continues to try to do in us is illegal.

Just as a gun may be used by its owner or the one who holds it to commit a crime, the gun is not bad or guilty of the crime. The court does not seek to rehabilitate the gun. In a similar fashion, the members of our bodies were being used to commit sin. They were not bad in themselves, any more than an instrument used to commit a crime is bad. The members of our body are not innately evil nor did they initiate the evil, though, in the hands and under the control of Evil, they will do Evil's bidding.

The big difference between the gun and humans, however, is that we are not inanimate objects. We have a free will to choose whom we will obey or believe or yield ourselves to. That is why the Scripture admonishes us to not permit or allow sin to rule over us. After we are reborn, we are free to choose to resist the temptation to yield our members to the works and wishes of Darkness. We now have a choice to yield ourselves to righteousness, though we still often seem to fall short of the ability to carry out those choices.

It is at this place of misery that we cry out like King David and the Apostle Paul, "Who will deliver me? Who will cause me to prevail against this Enemy who is too strong for me?" Jesus knew the battle would be ferocious and sent the Holy Spirit to live inside of us to protect us and teach us the truth. His work includes strengthening us to choose the truth and rejecting the lie in order to execute the freedom and liberty Christ died to give us.

Overcoming the Devil's lie begins by standing up against his counter arguments that challenge what we know to be true in our spirit. The battleground for sanctification is determined by whom we choose to believe and obey. In Romans 6:6, we see again what had emerged as a two-fold problem. We were slaves of the Devil, ruled by the Prince of Darkness. His takeover, however, was not just external.

We had been captured by something that had gotten inside of us. Like a cancer, the body of death was operating in our mind and in our members to get us to choose the lie and die. The cancer had to be destroyed without killing us (a challenge that many medical and religious interventions fail to do). It could only be accomplished by separating the sin (cancer) from the person.

The Law was unable to save us. It could only detect the cancer. It could only diagnose the disease. It was not the treatment or the cure for the disease or its effects in the body. Paul reminds us that "sin shall not (any longer) exert dominion over you, since now you are not under Law (as slaves), but under grace — as subjects of God's favor and mercy" (Romans 6:14 AMP).

Chapter 7

The Devil's Operating Software

The Body of Death operates like a cancer inside of us. We are built by God to live. Our emancipation from the powers of Hell could only be accomplished by removing the body of death. Just as surgery becomes the often-used method to remove a cancer, deliverance becomes God's method for removing the body of death operating system that controls us from within. We, however, are the ones who must give our permission before the surgeon can operate.

We have been given the power to yield to either God or the Devil. Our agreement determines the course of events. Our consent is as essential for the Kingdom of Darkness to move forward with its agenda to destroy us as it is for the Kingdom of God to move forward to free us. That consent, however, is not a one-time deal.

The scripture is quick to remind believers that if they continually surrender themselves to anyone to do his will, they will be the slaves of the one they obey. The possibility for getting stuck in our attempts to get free are as great as the number of times a day we must choose to stand our ground for God's truth. Failure to lay hold of the truth and obey God, or falling for the Enemy's lies, pull us deeper into the pit of doubt and despair.

Romans 6:16 makes it clear. The one rule of conquest in the contest between God and Satan for the souls of men is determined by whom we choose to believe and obey. Grace and forgiveness have been freely given and made available to us through the Cross. We died with Christ and thus, through death, have been translated out of the Kingdom of Darkness and into the Kingdom of the Son. We are no longer slaves of Darkness. The Lord God Himself has bought us off the auction block of Hell.

Though our spiritual repositioning into the Kingdom of God through salvation is both an earthly and a heavenly reality, it is not authenticated by how we feel. Our feelings do not validate or invalidate the work of salvation in us. "For we walk by faith, not by sight." (2 Cor. 5:7). If we rely on feelings to validate our faith, which many do, we will always be subject to the Enemy who would try to snatch away our salvation or mess with our hope every time we have a bad day.

Our freedom is established in the heavenly realm through faith in God's Word. Challenging our hearts to not believe God's promises becomes the Enemy's most persistent thrust. He desires to subvert the work of grace in us. Our faith must stand the test of continuing to rest upon the faithfulness of God in the face of the Devil's massive propaganda campaign to persuade us to think and feel differently.

Our legal release from the Kingdom of Darkness was accomplished through Death. Through our participation in Christ's death, we have been released from the Law and from those who would use the Law to obligate us. Dead men no longer pay taxes. They are not obligated to keep the contracts they made in life. Our contracts with sin and its ensuing death are cancelled out by the Cross.

The Court of God has pronounced us innocent and forgiven. Satan lost his legal jurisdiction over us; however, he still uses his manipulation of our circumstances to try and get us to waver in what God says about us and our freedom. All he has to do is to convince us that God is not real or that His Word is conditional. The Enemy uses our feelings and thoughts to continue to push against the gates of our fort and puncture our resistance. He is desperate to convince us that we are not saved. He uses our sin and failure to overcome the addiction as proof that we are not really saved or free. If we fall for his lies, he can bring us back into the pit of despair and loneliness. Using thoughts of doubt he plants into our minds himself, he convinces us that , "God was not there" and "I'm on my own."

The Word says, "For he who has died has been freed from sin." (Ro. 6:7). Now that we have been buried and declared to be dead we are also free to reckon our old man dead. We are loosed from Satan's internal domination. "Even so consider yourselves also dead to sin and your relation to it broken, but alive to God [living in unbroken fellowship with Him] in Christ Jesus." (Ro. 6:11 AMP).

Freedom

We are like the slaves who had been freed by the Emancipation Proclamation made by President Lincoln. They who had served as slaves were now free to get up and go from their place of slavery. They were free, but in order to enjoy that liberty they had to be delivered from the old mindsets attached to slavery and the patterns they had become used to.

They had physically been liberated. Now their old beliefs that had long before formed their concept of reality had to change if this newfound freedom was going to be real. Their thinking would have to be reprogrammed to facilitate a lifestyle of freedom. As it turned out, as free as they were on paper, they were still far from free in their hearts. For many, the change was too frightening, and they ended up staying in the comfort of the familiar, as painful as that had been. For some, venturing out into the big new world of freedom was not worth wrestling with all the unknowns that would come with it.

The transition into freedom for the believer happened by an act of God's proclamation, "It is finished." We are free and can rightly consider (reckon) ourselves not only dead to sin and our relationship with it broken, but alive unto God and welcomed into fellowship with Him. Is not this the whole point of the Gospel and the activity of God, to bring us into fellowship with Him?

That reckoning and our agreement with the work Christ did on the Cross now makes the Devil's work in us illegal. Through His death on the Cross, Jesus' work in us has accomplished what the pursuit of a better self could never do. Self-discipline cannot change our situation or set us free. The Cross released us from the dominion of Satan and our old life. We are no longer detained in the prison camps of Hell. We are no longer his rightful property as slaves of sin.

Slaves of Sin

In Romans 6:16–17, the Bible describes the determining point of the battle that rages between God and Satan for the souls of men. We are reminded that we become the slaves of the one we obey, either slaves to sin, which brings forth death, or slaves to righteousness, which brings forth life. Romans 6:17 continues the argument in the form of thanksgiving that reminds us that though we "were slaves of sin" we have since obeyed the doctrine of God, which has been brought to us. Freedom could only come through obedience to the Truth.

Obedience to the truth has set us free from the bondage to sin allowing us to become slaves unto righteousness. This form of slavery is voluntary. It becomes a pleasant walking in agreement with the Lord God and partaking in fellowship with Him. It is not a coercive manipulation of His Spirit contending with ours but rather a fulfilling of our divine purpose as His workmanship created in Christ Jesus unto good works.

But wait a minute! If I'm saved, why do I still find myself doing the things I hate? I am still sinning. What's up? I thought it was all taken care of at the Cross. I did what God said. I died with Christ. I want to be good, but I am still sinning. The things I do, I do not understand. What is not working in this plan of salvation and liberation?

Do Not Yield to Their Cravings!

In Romans 6:12, we are told to "not let sin reign in our mortal bodies, that we should obey it in its lusts." The Amplified Bible brings out even more meaning, adding the word *cravings* and personalizing it by putting the subject in a third person possessive. "Let not sin rule as king in your mortal, short-lived, perishable bodies, to make *you* yield to *their cravings* and be subject to *their* lusts and evil passions." (Ro. 6:12 AMP; emphasis added).

Do not continue offering or yielding your bodily members and faculties to sin as instruments (tools) of wickedness. But offer and yield your- selves to God as though you have been raised from the dead to (perpetual) life and your bodily members (and faculties) to God, presenting them as implements of righteousness." (Ro. 6:13 AMP)

The command is again clear. Do not let or permit the Devil to continue to bully you! We are free from his domain and the jurisdiction of the disembodied spirits from Hell that have set up their strongholds in our mortal body. From those strongholds they had taken over control of certain areas of our lives, thus giving sin the opportu- nity to reign in our flesh to create in us what Paul called a body of death. They were making us do things we did not want to do, that is, "to make us yield to their cravings." (See *Untangling the Lies of the Enemy* (two-CD set) www. liferecovery.com)

Who are "they" if *we* are the ones with the "perishable, short-lived bodies"? Whose cravings are we being warned to not accept? If sin rules as king, does that not imply there is a kingdom from which this king comes and a dominion which he would enforce? Could the cravings we are trying to minimize and control and overcome actually be a spiritual force within us that we are attempting to manage?

Managing Our Cravings

Romans 7 opens up the discussion in Chapter 6 further with Paul's own self-disclosure. We are reminded that "when we were living in the flesh (mere physical lives) … constantly operating in our natural powers, (in our bodily organs, in the sensitive appetites and wills of the flesh), so that we bore fruit for death" (Ro. 7:5, AMP), we were giving place to the weakness and vulnerabilities of our bodies. We were overcome by the pressure *Cravings* and *Lust* had put on us and were unable to live in freedom, though we had been declared to be free indeed (Jn. 8:36).

Through dying to the control of the kingdoms of this world, Jesus had set us free from Death in Romans 6, but here we are in Romans 7 still struggling within, still held captive by something inside of us that does not seem to want to let go. Even grace was not able to cause us to stop sinning, (Ro. 6:1). If dead men do not sin because they are not even tempted to sin, why are we still struggling with sin?

The only reasonable explanation is that though death had released us from the Kingdom of Darkness, God did not kill our physical bodies or take away our freedom to choose. Because we still have a free will we are still vulnerable to *Deception* and prone to slipping back under the influence of some internal program that directs us to continue to walk in the bondage we have become familiar with.

Just as freedom was illusive to the African slaves of the South, and the children of Israel who had been set free from the land of Egypt were still carrying Egypt in their hearts, we were still being internally controlled by the mindsets that had been formed through our experiences as slaves of Darkness. God would have to find a way to complete the internal liberation of our souls.

The Bible gives us a graphic description of what was going on. We read in the Amplified, "Having died to what once restrained and held us captive" (Romans 7:6 AMP). What is it that once *restrained and held us captive? "For sin, seizing the opportunity and getting hold on me ... beguiled, entrapped and cheated me...killed me"* (Romans 7:11 AMP; emphasis added). It sounds like someone or something had put us in a demonic headlock and body slammed us to the ground. How can any choice I make to act under the pressure of that kind of a struggle be considered an expression of my free will?

Romans 7:14 in the Amplified takes it deeper. "I am a creature of the flesh (carnal, unspiritual), having been sold into slavery under the control of sin." God warned Cain of sin's predatory nature saying, "Sin lies (crouches, KJV) at the door. And its desire is for you, but you should rule over it" (Gen. 4:7 KJV). God knew Cain had no idea of what he was up against. *Sin* is an evil intelligence with an agenda and its intention is to capture us.

Paul identifies sin in the same way. The thing that was in him was controlling his actions. His thoughts, feelings, and actions were being controlled by something other than his own intentions.

"For I do not understand my own actions—I am baffled, bewildered. I do not practice or accomplish what I wish, but I do the very thing that I loathe (which my moral instinct condemns)," (Ro. 7:15 AMP). He saw this thing in him acting contrary to his desire to keep the Law, which meant that he agreed with the Law that it was good. Looking at the Law had brought him clarity.

It not only made apparent that which had not been named or noticed, that is, the presence of sin, but it also gave Paul a standard with which to see his own character and intentions. Like the speed limit sign, it brought the offensive driving into the light. What was not defined before became definable. Sin and offense could not be identified until the Law laid down the line of transgression and judged the behavior as unacceptable.

What was wrong before now became an unmistakable violation. But in looking at the Law, Paul also saw something else. He saw that the Law was good and promoted justice. He concurred with that justice and desired to be found in conformity with it (Romans 7:15). The Law had become a mirror, showing Paul who he was. It gave him the opportunity to see a reflection of his divine nature in his agreement with the One who made him and the Law. He realized he never wanted to sin in the first place.

> For I know that nothing good dwells within me, that is, in my flesh. I can "want" what is right, but I cannot perform it.—I have the intention and urge to do what is right, but no power to carry it out." (Ro. 7:18 AMP)

The revelation melted away all the guilt and condemnation and striving he felt and brought him back to a place of goodness. It was not his intention or idea to sin in the first place. Paul seized the moment, in the midst of his battle with doing the thing he hated, to raise his voice in triumph and boldly proclaim; "Now if I do what I do not desire to do, it is no longer I doing it. It is not myself that acts, but the sin which dwells within me, fixed and operating in my soul." (Ro. 7:20 AMP).

He rounded out his observation by concluding that if it was not he himself doing it, then he was being subject to the insistent demands of something operating within him. Paul was admitting he had been imprisoned by the Enemy. He realized he was not in agreement or consenting with the sin. He also knew he did not want to do it. He was not confused about his intentions. If, then, he is not willfully doing the thing he found himself doing, he concluded that it is not him doing it, but the sin that dwelt in him. Though his bodily members were used to carry out the wishes of the force that controlled him, he attributed it to the war inside his members.

If we are subject to the insistent demands of the sin that dwells within us and the Enemy has taken control over our will and appetites, how is more willpower and taking more responsibility for that sin by "owning it" going to do much to free us? It would be like the prisoner of war who knows he is in captivity, held behind enemy lines, who thinks he can get free if he just *wants* his freedom bad enough when, in fact, the more he tries to get free the more he fails. The more he stresses over his freedom, the more drained and difficult it will be to endure or overcome the psychological and spiritual warfare needed to prevail against the obstacles.

Our freedom from sin has never been a matter of taking responsibility or using more willpower, from God's point of view. If our freedom would have been a matter of our "willpower" Our Lord never would have talked about His power to keep us from the power of the evil one who would try to snatch us from His hand. (See Jn. 10:28-29; Mt. 6:13). (Let us not misconstrue this to diminish our need to cooperate with God's grace and power to keep us through our obedience to Him). If Jesus would have told the disciples to try harder to be good and get it right, then grace would have been just a nice afterthought.

The Devil's ingenious plot is to make us think using our willpower and taking responsibility to overcome sin was God's idea when it really works well into the Devil's plan to tangle us up in works, religion, and guilt. He exercises control of our physiological organs using his body of death operating software to get us to believe a lie. We choose the lie under the intimidation of fear and deception, and sin.

He then convinces us we are guilty (it is entirely our fault) or gets us to blame someone else and agree that we, or they, deserve to be punished. We accept the consequences as a divine judgments coming against us because of our sin. We feel guilty and are motivated to do penance or take responsible to get rid of the sin in order to be absolved and feel better.

The guilt and shame and pain motivate us to fix ourselves and re-establish our goodness through better behavior. But, because we can never be good enough and can never do it right enough to please the Devil, peace and a sense of well-being constantly elude us. We feel doomed into never feeling free or forgiven. Self-effort and "working the program," be it spiritual or secular becomes the perfect trap!

- How have you been imprisoned by your attempts to quit using and be free?

Chapter 8

The Torture Rack of Responsibility

What an epiphany in Paul's life! What an incredibly liberating moment for Paul to realize he could not take the responsibility for doing the things he did not want to do because he was not the one who was doing that thing he hated. "Now if I do what I will not to do, it is no longer I who do it, but sin that dwells in me." (Ro. 7:20). He realized his "will" and volition were not in agreement with the thing sin was doing in him.

He realized that for the thing to be a valid act attributed to his free will he would have had to have been free to act. Not only had he made no agreement with it, the thing had coerced him by controlling his actions. He was not in control of the thing he saw himself doing; therefore, he concluded it was not him doing it! He could not take responsibility for doing something he was forced to do because he was being controlled by something that had overpowered his free will.

Just as remarkable as is this statement, is the absence of any Divine correction of Paul's conclusion. God does not interrupt him at this point or instruct Paul to delete or rewrite Romans 7:20 to demand that his readers to take responsibility for their actions. God does not correct the inspired record by reminding Paul, or us, that the action was made by our free will, and because we chose, we must take responsibility for the transgression and own up to it or be guilty as charged. He does not even demand we change by trying another approach.

The aftershock of Paul's discovery prompts him to ask a rhetorical question. Should we "continue in sin that grace might abound?" Would we pervert grace by taking advantage of God's good will and Heaven's mercy to cast His mercies back in His face with our arrogant ingratitude or presumptuous disobedience? The very fact that Paul asks the question about continuing in sin even after experiencing grace would confirm to us that neither sin nor grace had taken away our free will. There must still be something in operation that was controlling our will against our will.

In spite of the thousands of times the Bible records mankind's sin in turning from his Creator and the corresponding opportunities God took to set the biblical record straight, none are summarized as an admonition for us to take responsibility for our sin. The Bible called for obedience. Obedience brought divine protections and blessing to the people. The responsibility God is looking for from us is to repent and trust Him with an obedient heart. Repentance and obedience are critical in turning the people back to God as can be seen in the opening statement that Jesus made in launching His public ministry when He said, "Repent, for the Kingdom of Heaven is at hand" (Mt. 4:17).

Some might argue that to be obedient is the same as to be responsible. The Bible makes little mention of taking responsibility as a necessary gesture on our part to prove our sincerity or sorrow for sin. The necessary responsibility the Word of God requires us to take is to trust in the faithfulness of God our Heavenly Father. Repentance essentially and simply means to "change your mind." And if the lie *Fear* is telling us is at the root of our choice to sin, changing our minds and believing the truth about God's love and faithfulness becomes the first and most responsible thing we can do.

Looking for the Admonition

In studying the Gospels and Christ's interaction with the disciples, we do not find Him scolding them for making a mistake or correcting them by telling them they need to take responsibility. Did He rebuke them for forgetting to bring bread the day after the feeding of the 5,000? Did He take the opportunity to tell them they should have been more responsible? Did He greet Peter after he denied Him three times by telling him he needed to take responsibility for his actions and apologize to the group? Did He correct the Sons of Thunder, James and John, for wanting to call down fire on the Samaritans by telling them it was immature and irresponsible?

Taking responsibility is a humanistic word used to place blame and motivate us to do things. "It's up to me to fix it" is the common, typically recommended approach to solving problems. But whose recommendation are we following—God's or the Enemy's? Taking responsibility is our "knee jerk," natural reaction to most everything that goes wrong in our life and is a useful tool in the Enemy's arsenal. With it, he would hinder the growth of our love for God and others and bind us with blame and shame and judgment of one another.

God never asks us to get into the "boxing ring" with Satan to prove our worth or good intentions because He knows we are no match for the wiles of the Devil. We are lured into the arena to fight the gladiators of Hell who would challenge our identity, our actions, and our righteousness. Because life is an arena full of problems, we are constantly tempted to take back the task of solving our life-of-sin problems ourselves, the antithesis to trusting in God.

The Torture Rack of Hell

Everywhere we turn, we are being taught to take responsibility, to "grow up," "use our brain," "don't be stupid," "get it right," and "just do something"! We are surrounded with both the spoken and the unspoken expectations to be responsible and carry the burden of their demands wherever we go. Responsibility carries with it the hidden agenda that compels us to join the rat race of life and live on the torture rack of Hell.

One of the Enemy's favorite strategies is to pull us apart by setting us up to solve the irresolvable conflicts of life. We get strapped and trapped on the torture rack between "trying harder" and "it's never enough." He uses our desire for freedom to catch us between *Cravings* and the need to control those cravings. How many have become rich selling other men a remedy for their pain as a "proven method" to escape from the torture racks from Hell only to be tricked by another false hope?

Let me clarify, for all who might be angry or shocked at what they are reading. Some of you may never have read anything like this before. Some of you are not sure what you are reading. And for others, some of what you are reading is not what I am saying. I am not advocating that we give ourselves permission to act irresponsibly in disregarding the good of others. I am *not* excusing us from doing that which is right with reasons like, "I cannot help myself" or "I'm not responsible" or because "I have a demon."

What I am saying is that "all the law is fulfilled in this, that we "love one another." (Gal. 5:14). The Law of love takes us beyond the Ten Commandments or the law of civic duty and responsibility to the place of truth and sacrifice. Taking responsibility apart from love is merely the Devil's argument to justify placing huge burdens of guilt on us to force us further into the wilderness of sin, *Confusion,* and *Despair.* Responsibility becomes the whip the Enemy uses to drive us, like a flock of frightened sheep, away from God's green pastures, over the cliffs of self-destruction and efforts to try harder, until we are dashed on the rocks of "never enough" because "nothing ever changes."

Failure and *Condemnation* wait at the bottom of the precipice of responsibility to devour those who have come into agreement with Hell's henchmen of *Guilt* and *Condemnation.* We feel lost and alone, unworthy and unaware of the love of God. We feel unfit for the Kingdom regardless of the sacrifice Jesus Christ made to qualify us to get there. We feel like we are hung out to dry, strung up between *Doubt* and a "need" to do more. Our hope to see the goodness of God in the land of the living is lost and the kingdom of God vanishes from sight.

Can God Contradict Himself?

Though the Bible is replete with examples of man's sin and our analysis of man's need to be responsible for his sin, God could not take this humanistic approach in making man responsible for his own sin without contradicting Himself. How could God tell us that we all need a Savior because we cannot be good enough to satisfy the demands of sin and then turn around and tell us we need to be good to get to Heaven?

God cannot tell us that we all have sinned and there is none righteous and that there is none good but God, (Mk. 10:18), and then turn around and set up keeping the Law as the criterion for righteousness and salvation unless He is willing to deny His own Word.

He does not demand we take responsibility for sin that we are not in agreement with committing any more than we would hold a kidnapped child responsible as an accomplice to their own kidnapping. We would not call them irresponsible for being captured even if they had been warned not to go with strangers, nor would we allow them to remain in jeopardy if we had the power to deliver them to safety.

"But I disobeyed," you say. "I *did* want to do it." Yes, and the child did disobey their parent's instructions and did want the candy being offered by the kidnapper to get into the car. So does being tricked by the Devil make the whole thing now my fault and the one who deceived me guiltless? At what place does forgiveness and restoration begin, if not at the place where it is needed the most?

At what place would rescue or ransom ever be a legitimate part of God's plan if we could have earned our own way to heaven? If we could have been good enough, Salvation would have become something earned as opposed to something given. Redemption would have canceled itself out as a meaningless act like giving our whole life's wages in exchange for our freedom to be able to work our whole life to earn wages we needed to pay our own debts.

We cannot have it both ways and neither can God. Jesus Christ is the Way, the only Way, to God. Sin is not the deterrent to entering heaven. Rejecting Christ is. Salvation is not about being good or doing things right. It is not a question of taking responsibility or taking the blame or doing penance to undo the sin or doing good to make up for it. It is receiving grace and forgiveness and our restoration to the Father.

Sin sold us into slavery and holds us captive against our will. Sin demanded a ransom. The ransom was not made with gold and silver or putting money in the offering plate. It was made with blood. Blood had to be given for blood shed. Death had to be given for the life that was taken. Death had to be satisfied. "The soul who sins shall die" (Ez. 18:20), and the "life of the flesh is in the blood." (Lev. 17:11). The only blood left that did not already belong to the Devil was the Blood of the Son of God made flesh. His Blood was the only currency with fair market value that could be traded in the Universal System of Justice for the legal exchange of a man's soul. A man sinned. A man must die.

Because of Adam's sin, we were already prisoners, born enslaved by the Evil One. Our blood was not ours to give, though the Devil delights greatly in the spilling of it. Only the Blood of One free from the beginning, whose soul was not held in slavery to the god of this world system, could come down and enter the world to give His Blood to satisfy the demands of Death. (See *Setting Captives Free* (Manual) www.liferecovery.com.)

Hell's Demonic Mandates: Religion, Reasoning, Reality, and Responsibility

The Devil could not stop God's plan of redemption in His determination to rescue fallen man with His generous gift of salvation. All the Devil could do was interfere with it. The easiest way he found to interrupt it was to reinterpret it. *Religion, Reasoning, Reality,* and *Responsibility* all volunteered to rewrite the constitution of human freedom based on a platform of good works. They succeeded in lobbying for the minor changes that fit nicely with man's divine sensitivity to imperfection and innate hatred for sin.

All the Devil had to do was shift the focus to the sin, and the Son would be wonderfully obscured! He would use sin and the pain of our separation from God as a motivator to get us to do whatever it took to "get back to God." He would then come in to befriend us. The Enemy, guised to be our counselor and protector, would comfort and guide us through our wretched state of sin and separation, to help us get "closer to God."

This time he would take up the form, not of a talking Serpent, but of a talking self, an inner voice that would seduce and deceive us. The *Angel of light* had outdone himself! He had thought of everything. The plot of planting the thoughts in the mind of man was more successful than he could have even imagined, (though his imagination was only evil continually). All that was left to do was to cross his fingers and hope that we would never suspect, at least not until it was too late to make a difference, who was really behind the grand lie that inspired us in our efforts to stop sinning and be free.

Man, having been given a free will by the Creator Himself, made the scheme a seamless masterpiece. Free will would make them completely accountable for every move they made and thus fully chargeable for everything they did wrong. Everything hinged on who was responsible. His goal was within easy reach. He would get them to feel responsible for everything they did. Getting them to take responsibility for things they did not even do themselves would be a bonus.

Our keen sense of right and wrong including our hatred of sin and our susceptibility to shame made us perfect targets for the fiery darts of *Guilt* and the thoughts of "I should have" that *Guilt* had implanted. We were already feeling so bad about what had happened in the Garden that it would be a piece of cake for the Tempter to make us feel responsible for what could have happened, what should have happened, what did not happen, and everything that did. Everything would be our fault. He would make us believe that every shoe in *Guilt's* shoe store fit us. He would even get us to feel responsible and guilty for things that were done to us, including vile and abusive things we had no power to stop or take control of in the first place.

Chapter 9

Guilt: One Size Fits All

The question of "whose responsibility is it" made guilt universally assignable. The charges would be irrefutable. Even the youngest child could now be charged with heinous crimes that they would not be able to refute. The establishment of their true identity and intention would be lost in their endless attempts to prove their innocence by trying to change. The lies would begin at conception. The accusations would be programmed into their very soul. The voice of the *Accuser* would be their constant companion in the day and their relentless haunting in the night.

Works, good deeds, and taking responsibility—who would ever see through any of it enough to protest the Enemy's plot against grace and God's unspeakable gift of love and forgiveness? Confronting them with their own misdeeds would confound them and keep them from knowing the power of God's love. It would destroy them and forever make God look like an idiot for loving them. It was Satan's plan and it was perfect.

In switching the emphasis onto being good and earning salvation, the Enemy could laugh in the face of every man who fell for the lie that he must prove himself worthy of love and eternal life. Knowing full well that a master does not owe his slaves anything, no matter how hard the slave works to earn it, the Devil intended to keep them enslaved by their own good deeds. By very virtue of being a slave, the enslaved has given over to his master the right to his life, his posterity, and all of his productivity.

We were slaves of sin. There was nothing we could do about that. We needed to be rescued, ransomed, and redeemed. We needed to be bought back by the One who loved us enough to prove it. Goodness and chivalry and justice are not any of Satan's strong character suits. He has mercy on no one.

All through the years of human generation, *Death* and *Destruction* have worked hand in hand with *Responsibility* and *Religion* to conceal their intentions. The wasting eye of *Destruction* and the skeleton of *Death* wait patiently for the reaping of our souls as we anxiously consume ourselves with the burden of trying to medicate our pain and mend our circumstances.

Torn between the sin we hate and taking responsibility to do better, we build our case for righteousness on the Devil's recommendations only to find our efforts getting thrown out of Heaven's Court of Appeals on grounds of practicing lawlessness (See Mt.7:21–23). The Enemy's lies are as relentless as his arguments are convincing.

We have no way to refute the evidence. We did sin. It was our choice. We did fail to keep our promise. We did feel or think or do that thing we hate. As he continues to build his case against us, the evidence of our sin mounts up, convincing us he is right. We have no defense against such a clever argument. We lose hope of ever seeing ourselves vindicated or restored. Surrendering to the prosecution appears to be our only choice. (See *It's My Fault* (CD) www.liferecovery.com)

The Devil's Plan of Salvation

In this helpless state, the Devil comes to "assist" us. His plan of "salvation" is crafted to help us regain our lost righteousness and restore justice. He comes to us guised as any number of religious attempts to appease God and make amends. Because we are eager to get closer to God, we are duped into doing what Hell's experts on holiness recommend, including the use of rituals, self-punishment, penance, and behavior modification.

The thrust of his devilish plan is driven by both *Guilt* and the need to take responsibility for our sin. *Guilt* motivates us to pursue our salvation and the forgiveness of sin by working for grace through any number of rituals and religious practices: practices that can never make the practitioner perfect or free.

Works in and of themselves don't work. When we work to earn our righteousness, it makes God obligated to us. He becomes a debtor to us as we opt to change the qualifications of redemption from grace to works. Salvation becomes a matter of wages owed. God becomes, not the Merciful Savior, but the boss. That's when Satan has succeeded in getting us to believe another lie, undermining the character of God and the grace He has so freely given.

Salvation is not a matter of taking responsibility or deserving. It is a gift that has been freely given by love and received by faith. The only true interpretation of the Gospel message is given as one of "faith which works by love" (Gal. 5:6) and grace. Though many of the current versions of the gospel use human effort and self as part of the salvation equation, all other renditions of the Gospel than the one Christ brought as expounded on by the apostle Paul are counterfeits. They are based on man's interpretation of God and His Word reconstructed and misconstrued under the influence of the Enemy.

Any gospel not understood through "faith that works by love" (Gal. 5:6) will ultimately reduce our concept of God to that of a distant despot. What better way to further the Devil's alienation process between us and our Heavenly Father than to promote the stress and striving of a gospel of good works. Works and self-sanctification promote a salvation based on *Fear*. *Fear* creates a salvation sustained by works. The vicious cycle is fueled by our fervor in an attempt to be "responsible" to stop sinning and at the same time we attempt to not feel guilty for not being good. (Sin must be acknowledged and dealt with according to God's provisions, not the Devil's. Admission, repentance, confession, and humbling ourselves before God bring forgiveness and healing).

Fear is not a good motivator in relationships where love is the desired outcome. Though breaking the Law caused Paul pain, it was not his pain or his fear of going to Hell that prompted Paul in recognizing who he was or what was going on. The Law caused him to realize that he did not want to sin. The Law became the looking glass in which he caught his own reflection. His inner man was in agreement with the goodness of the Law. The Law was a reflection of the intentions of God. When

Paul realized that his intentions were the same as God's, he was shocked and overjoyed! At that moment he saw clearly the snare his soul was in, caught up in doing something he himself hated!

Pulling Ourselves Out of the Magician's Hat

Trying to discover our true identity and intention, or trying to justify our behavior, or accepting Jesus Christ as our Savior based on the fear of going to Hell or in an effort to relieve our pain, is like trying to pull ourselves out of a magician's hat. It's like trying to catch our reflection in a muddy pool. *Fear* gives us no assurance that our motives are right and thus no clear reflection of who we are. Paul's discovery of his agreement with God's law came out of seeing his reflection in the perfect law of liberty. He knew he was free from condemnation in spite of the wretchedness he felt churning in his soul and the war he saw raging in his members.

He knew he could not ever defend himself or his actions based on his excuses or a resolve to do better. He came into agreement with God in spite of his actions, making an even stronger case for the distinction between his being and his behavior. He was free in his spirit. In his soul, he was condemned. He did not attempt to justify his behavior or minimize it. He was more than content to recognize that he resonated with the intentions of God and that his relationship with God was not based upon good behavior but upon being created in the image of God. All he knew was that he wanted God, and God wanted him.

If our salvation is initially birthed in fear, it must eventually be transplanted into the sweet soil of God's love or our little roots will shrivel in the Devil's acidic demands about the need to be good enough to stay saved. The revelation of Paul's agreement with God was based not on fear but on recognition of the similitude between him and God. That revelation allowed him to see that it was not he who wanted to sin.

Once Paul realized he did not want to sin, he began to see clearly the war going on inside of him to separate him from himself was separate from him. Agreeing with the evidence presented by the Enemy would only succeed in making that separation more painful and permanent. No longer did the Enemy's argument convince him he was responsible and it was his fault he was still doing the thing he hated. The misery of his sin and the wretchedness of his condition had opened his eyes to the need for deliverance.

He embraced the Law as good. He was on the side of good and wanted that which was good. His intentions were clarified by the Law in spite of the Enemy's use of the law to present the evidence of his sin against Paul and use his feelings of guilt and condemnation to convince him that he was bad. Paul knew the truth; he did not want to sin! He was no longer caught in the dilemma, pulled between the thing he did and the thing he did not seem to have the power to stop doing. Desire and intention defined volition. Volition and his will were solidly on the side of God and good.

Not only did the Law give Paul a look at his true identity, it allowed him to see what was holding him captive. The thing he had been afraid to look at before, he now closely examined. Sin had made its home in him and taken possession of him (Ro. 7:17). He could humbly cry out with relief, "who will deliver me from this body of death?"

The Law as a Temporary Stay of Execution

Paul clearly understood that the Law could only give those who kept it a temporary stay of execution from *Death*. It had no power to remove their guilt or save them. The Bible is clear. The Law was not given to deliver us or forgive us. It was a temporary covering and protection used in identifying the children of God, not a method to cancel out sin. The Law was given by God to provide a temporary extension of amnesty until the final sacrifice, the Lamb of God, would come to take away the sins of the world.

Jesus Christ's sacrifice released us from the continual offering of the lamb's blood demanded by the Law of the Old Testament. It made those sacrifices obsolete. Until the fullness of time had come, all the Law could do for those who kept it was to keep them safe from the Devil's demands for their immediate execution. His accusations that they deserved to die would have to wait for the Day of Judgment. Their obedience in pledging their allegiance to God and faith in His promises through the keeping of the Law secured their right to be protected by God until the final sacrifice was made. Through that sacrifice those who faithfully followed the Lord would also be found delivered from the judgment of sin and death on that final Day.

Even though the Law was good as a temporary covering, only the grace of God as given in the New Testament could bring full and final forgiveness and freedom to the enslaved. Paul began to see that his need was for more than an external rescue. He saw the freedom he longed for would have to include an internal emancipation as well.

No Willpower against It

But what was that thing that was obstructing his freedom to follow God? Only when Paul heard himself cry out, "Who will deliver me from this body of death" did he realize he had named it. He had called this internal operating system "the Body of Death." He realized that the demonic forces behind his behavior were contrary to the Law and God's intentions in giving it.

He realized that even though he knew he had no desire to sin, he seemed to have no power to stop it. He lamented that he had "no willpower against it, no power to carry out his will ..." (Ro. 7:18). If my desire is not consenting to the sin I am doing and I do not want to do it, then Paul concludes, "It must not be me." Therefore, that thing which acts in me, as me, is not me, "but the sin which dwells in me, fixed and operating in my soul," (Ro.7:20 AMP). Paul laments saying, "and I am subject to its insistent demands ..." (Ro. 7:21 AMP).

Paul was not making excuses for his behavior. He was not denying it or defending it. He wanted to deal with it while realizing that the war within was out of control. "I discern in my bodily members—the sensitive appetites and wills of the flesh—a different law (rule of action) at war against the law of my mind ... making me a prisoner of the law of sin that dwells in my bodily organs—in the sensitive appetites and wills of the flesh." (Ro. 7:23 AMP).

The battle had spread to his appetite and his will. The revelation that Paul had received moments earlier now allowed him to see that though his will and desire were missing from the equation, the fact that his volition was missing was not enough to get the sin to quit. It did not seem to be enough to stop the insistent demands of this thing that controlled his bodily organs and appetites simply because he did not want to do it.

His body was vulnerable. There were certain things he needed to have to live. Somehow something had gotten control over him. The thing was not even affected by his determination to not be controlled by it. Even his willpower to overcome it was being dismantled. In recognizing that this thing was stronger than his puny efforts to dislodge it, he realized he was like a prisoner being held hostage in his own soul.

He was a free man who was still enslaved. How could this be? Was he like Houdini who sat in the prison cell, believing he had been bolted in, only to discover that the door to the chamber had never even been locked? In assuming the obvious he had missed the actual truth. Not realizing we are free or failing to believe and declare we are free because we do not see or feel the evidence of that freedom, creates its own kind of imprisonment.

"Oh, wretched man that I am!" becomes the cry of many who sincerely desire to be free. *Reality* tells me I am still bound. The Truth says I am free. But if I still see myself sinning how can I be free? I begin to hate myself for doing what I hate and not getting the victory. My friends make their suggestions. My sponsors hold me accountable. My support groups get tired of waiting for me to shape up. I cannot hide my sin any longer and the scale never lies. *Guilt* is "eating me up." I sit in *Confusion,* trying to ward off the accusations and fight the feelings of

Shame as best I can, while I muster enough faith to stay in the race and try again.

(See *Taking the Devil to Court* (Book) www.liferecovery.com.)

- What assumptions have you made about the addictions that hold you captive?

Chapter 10

What's Wrong with
This Picture?

W hat's wrong with this picture? If the Bible clearly
tells us we are being controlled by sin, how will
any amount of willpower or self-discipline or self-control or dieting or program-based solutions be able to set
us free from bondage to that sin? We go with our feelings. We regard our thoughts as our own. The opinions
of experts and self-appointed authorities not only misdi-
agnose our condition, but also misjudge us in the situation, bringing perpetual confusion about what needs to
be done to remedy it.

We cannot seem to separate ourselves from our
behavior or the consequences of that behavior, which
only causes us to work harder to try to overcome the sin.
Because we were taught to believe we must manage our
thoughts and control our feelings, we try again.

The Word of God is "sharper than any two-edged
sword" (Heb.4:12), able to discern the difference between

our behavior and our being. It is able to consistently separate the temptations, which include our thoughts and feelings, from the intentions to act upon those thoughts. The Word of God is able to do what we are not! It separates us from the thoughts and feelings springing up out of the soul and sets us free to know the truth. The Word of God is a surgical instrument in the hand of the Lord that is able to separate us, our will and intentions, from our behavior.

> The Word of God is living and powerful, and sharper than any two-edged sword, piercing even to the division of the soul and spirit, and of the joints and marrow, and is a discerner of the thoughts and intents of the heart. (Heb. 4:12)

Only the Word of God has the wisdom and discretion to separate our thoughts from our intentions to act upon those thoughts.

Not Every Thought You Think You Thought

Not every thought you think you thought are thoughts you thought. Some of the thoughts you think you thought are temptations, ideas, and suggestions dressed up like your own thoughts, filtered through your own mind by the *Tempter,* who disguises them to look and sound and feel like you so he can get you to embrace them as your own. Because we are often confused as to where the temptation stops and the intention to act upon the temptation starts, we are easy targets for *Confusion* and *Condemnation.*

Only God truly knows our hearts. Even when our hearts condemn us and we are confused, which God knows Satan will seek to do, God knows all things. He is the ultimate judge of my heart. (1 Jn. 3:19–21). He reserves the right to overrule me even in the judgments I've made against myself, in order to uphold the truth. He votes *for* me. He knows my intentions and my desire to want to do what is right. He knows the wiles of the Devil. Even when Satan sets me up to agree with him in condemning myself and saying that I am stupid and never going to get it right, God knows the truth.

Self-Condemnation and Despair

Has the war within turned into a daily battle? The Bible describes that war as a wrestling "not against flesh and blood, but against principalities, powers, the rulers of the darkness of this age and the spiritual hosts of wickedness in heavenly places" (Eph. 6:12).

The fight can be over anything, over what to eat or drink or what not to eat or drink. It is anything around which the Enemy can instigate a riot, raise an argument, or create division or a dispute. The dispute could be over our salvation, our righteousness, or our responsibility.

The battle begins as a debate between our soul and our spirit. The temptation comes into our soul as a thought or a feeling. The Accuser can address it as an act of omission or commission. The question of intentions sets up the spiritual fight that creates a useful division between our soul and our spirit. All internal debates are inspired by Hell to "divide the house" (Mt. 12: 25) and set me up in "opposition to myself" (2 Tim. 2: 25 KJV). His intention is to make me doubt who I am or the validity of my salvation. His goal is to cause me to waver in my resolve, undermine my courage, and intimidate me until I give in and accept the Enemy's accusations as true.

The Disguise

The opposition of the Enemy often comes to us as a thought disguised by the Enemy to be our own. In his attempt at identity theft, and as a thief, he is attempting to switch out his thoughts and feelings for ours. This makes him a first-person impersonator. Jesus called him the *"Strong man"* in Matthew 12:29. The thought, the feelings and the temptation to act upon those thoughts and feelings come to us guised as our own, making it hard for us to discern the difference between what is truly and rightly part of who I am and what is the demonic pseudo-recreation of the "I am" that looks and feels and sounds like me. Because most of us do not even consider this level of conspiracy against our lives, we disregard any such activity, if indeed, we notice it at all.

Failing to quickly and clearly distinguish the real "I am" created in the image of God from the counterfeit look-alike imitation impersonation of me can create immediate and serious problems. *Division* and *Confusion* rise up inside of me. *Doubt* and *Double-mindedness* set in. I am uncertain about my motives, and I feel like a hypocrite. Failing to discern the difference between my being and my behavior makes me edgy and defensive. I try to protect myself against the Devil's accusations, only to be cornered into a defenseless position by his cunningly twisted perversion of the truth.

If we fail to differentiate between the Devil's temptation and accusation and our intention to act on the temptation, we will assume the guilt of a sin we were only "tempted" to commit. Because there are many sins of the mind, the Enemy slides in the thoughts he presents to our mind as our own. We accept the blame for having thought those thoughts even though we had no desire or intention to do or think those thoughts.

Only the Sword of the Word is sharp enough to separate a thought from an intention to act upon that thought (Heb.4:12). If we fail to recognize our need for deliverance and try to set ourselves free by making a greater resolve to control our mind instead of "taking every thought captive," we will be caught in the endless trap of mental anguish, full of S*triving, Anxiety,* and *Obsession. Failure* is the desired outcome and ultimate end of every argument C*ondemnation* makes against us. His goal is to crush us under the feet of *Despair.* Only a cry like Paul's, "O wretched man that I am, who will deliver me?" can change the inevitable outcome of *Defeat* and set us free.

That's It! I Quit!

At that point of human desperation the Word of God does not expect us to do another thing. It does not instruct us to "try harder" or "get over it" or look for another program or buy another product or find a better mentor. The Bible offers the desperate only one solution. Paul cried out not, "What more must I do," but "Who will deliver me?" The solution is not in another what or how or self-help or special diet or the discovery of secret knowledge; it is in knowing *I need deliverance* and in knowing *who it is that can deliver me.*

I need a Deliverer. I need someone to set me free from *Failure, Guilt, Self-hatred,* and *Sin.* I need One who will deliver me from this state of feeling out-of-control that *Craving* has set up inside of me to look like "me." That pseudo-self, the counterfeit of me, is pressuring me with this urge to use, or eat, or practice doing the thing I hate. I need One who can deliver me from the war that rages inside of me to defeat the division that is working to divide my house and set my soul up in opposition against my spirit (2 Tim. 2:24–26).

No Condemnation

Paul continues his question. "Who will deliver me from this 'body of death'"? What is a body of death? The body of death has become the operating software the Enemy has been using to control us. The body of sin and the body of death were downloaded into us at the Fall when Adam and Eve came into agreement with the Devil. Now Paul cries out, asking *who* will deliver him from the war that rages inside of his members?

Just as quickly as Paul cries out, he realizes that Christ Jesus has, not will, but *has* done it! "Therefore, (there is) *now* no condemnation, no adjudging guilty of wrong (doing) to those who are in Christ Jesus, who live not after the dictates of the flesh, but after the dictates of the Spirit" (Ro. 8:1 AMP). When is "now"? Now is right this second, where you are, sitting there reading this sentence. Now is not when you get your act together or after you get sober or when you lose twenty-five pounds.

"Now" is now, and the truth is that even in our unperfected state, if we are in Christ Jesus, we are free from condemnation! Those who have come into agreement with Jesus Christ are set free from the curses that come with the agreements made with the Evil One if they choose to walk in the Spirit. What an incomprehensible thought since it goes so contrary to the evidence we have received from the Accuser. Being in Christ Jesus is the only reason I am in this state of blessed acquittal.

Who is this one, then, who acts as a dictator of the flesh? What is the flesh? The answers to these questions hold the key to unraveling the mystery of the war within. The definition of the flesh is often misunderstood and swapped out for the general list of sins, lust, adultery, uncleanness, licentiousness, idolatry, sorcery, and so forth contained in Galatians 5:19–21. A closer reading, however, identifies these as the works of the flesh, not the flesh itself.

The flesh is the fearfully and wonderfully made vessel that carries the soul and spirit around. Some would argue that "in my flesh dwells no good thing" (Ro. 7:18). We must remember that something dwelling in my house is neither my house nor me. Can I have a rat in my house? Does having a rat in my house make me a rat? Does having a spirit of *Craving* in my house make me a spirit of *Craving,* or am I, in fact, being controlled by one?

It is interesting to note that the way the scripture reads in Romans 8:1–2, it is possible to both be saved and feel condemned at the same time. Paul is describing the war that goes on in our flesh, that is, the functioning of our soul and the body together, against our spirit. To avoid the confusion and the condemnation that comes out of mixing reasoning, feeling, and thinking, all resident operations of our soul, with our spirit, Paul reminds us to walk according to the Spirit.

From these passages it would appear that we can be saved and yet feel condemned at the same time if we continue to choose to walk in the flesh. Being saved and feeling saved are two different things. We are *not* saved based upon our feelings of being saved any more than our salvation is based upon seeing God with our natural eyes. Faith is not based on sight (what things look like) (2 Cor. 5:7). Faith comes from believing what God said!

Who or What Do You Believe?

Our salvation is based upon our faith in the fact that God says we are saved and God cannot lie. "For every one who calls upon the name of the Lord (invoking Him as Lord) will be saved." (Ro. 10:13 AMP). Salvation is our position in Christ. Still doing the things we hate after we are saved merely describes the battle between the new spiritual man and the old carnal man. The question is not what am I doing or how am I feeling, but who am I believing? Is my eternal security based on what I see myself doing or what God says?

The good news is I do have victory in the finished work of Jesus Christ, and I can know I have that victory if I choose to listen to and follow what God said. Jesus commanded His disciples to follow Him (Mt. 4:19). We are to walk in the Spirit and abide in the True Vine. As a branch, I am fully supplied with all that I need to live a life pleasing to God.

Abiding in Him allows the Spirit of God to flow through me to support me and guide my spirit. I no longer live according to the old methods of the soul, thinking and feeling my way through life. Instead, I walk in the confidence of knowing that God's Spirit is directing me and bears witness with my spirit. Knowing that we know what is going on is the last thing the Devil wants us to know and the first thing we must know to walk in freedom and stay in victory.

- What is the war that rages within your soul that makes you miserable?
- The Word of God says, "You will keep him in perfect peace whose mind is stayed upon You, because he trusts in You." (Is. 26:3) What are the thoughts and feelings that keep your mind and heart afraid and anxious?

Chapter 11

The Internal Takeover

Of course the Devil uses every opportunity to raise any question that might bring *Doubt* or *Confusion* into the relationship we have with our Lord Jesus Christ. How saved am I? If I am a believer can I lose my salvation? I don't feel saved, so how can I be sure I am abiding or when will I be good enough or how do I know if I am in the will of God?

If we remember the Devil's basic strategy is to divide and conquer, then it all makes perfect sense. His goal is to set us in opposition to ourselves (2 Tim.2:24–26 KJV). He gets us to use our soul to navigate through life. The Soul Software comes as the standard operating system for every living human being. It is designed to rely on the Self and works contrary to walking in the Spirit.

The Enemy begins his internal takeover by tempting our mind to *Doubt* and our heart to *Fear*. He works to set up his argument in our soul to undermine the revelation of God's Holy Spirit made known to our spirit. Our spirit is the "candle of the Lord searching all the inner rooms of the heart." (Pr. 20:27). That candle gets lit when we get saved.

The candle was lit by the Light of the World who paid the price for the liberty we now enjoy as we walk in the Spirit. His Blood paid the purchase price *Death* was asking of us. In that purchase God both satisfied the demands made upon us by sin and death and defeated its work in us. The Death of Christ condemned sin in the flesh and rendered *Death* and *Destruction's* hold on us as illegal and impotent. This makes it entirely possible for us to walk in the Spirit and please God.

When we accept the offering God has made on our behalf, we are set free from the grip of the Evil One. The works of *Darkness* in us have become illegal though Satan does not automatically or immediately leave just because the King bought the house. Just like the thief does not stop robbing banks just because robbing banks has been declared to be illegal, the rat continues to occupy the house that he does not own as long as he can.

God fulfilled the requirements of the very Law the Devil was using to indict us. The Devil needs the Law and uses its prestige to accuse us of wrongdoing in the sight of God. We feel guilty and succumb to its charges. When we fail to appreciate the liberty we have been given in Christ (Gal. 5:1), the Enemy uses the Law, and his position as the Accuser of the Brethren to maintain his control over us.

The Lord God, on the other hand, recognized our susceptibility to the lies of the Accuser and circumvented the weaknesses of our flesh by taking the matter of our salvation out of our hands and doing it Himself. He knew we would never be able or qualified to take on the demands sin had put upon us, so He did it for us with one caveat: our agreement. Because our free will was a necessary part of the "whosoever" invitation, we had to be given the right to accept or reject God's free gift of salvation.

How silly to think that some would choose to reject such an offer because it was too good to be true or too easy or wasn't the religious persuasion they had been raised in. However, we know that because the Devil is who he is, in his cunning he has convinced more than a few to pass on the Lord God's offer of eternal life. For all those who do accept His sacrifice and free gift of salvation, the matter of sin is finished. God has "subdued, overcome, and deprived sin of its power" (Ro. 8:3 AMP). We are now free if we want to be. The choice is ours. The line of demarcation has been drawn between slaves and sons, with the options to either as real as the stakes are eternal.

The problem of acting on a future promise, however, is that the influence of the immediate experience is usually more persuasive than the call of a distant promise of eternal life.

For those who are according to the flesh and controlled by its unholy desires, set their mind on and pursue those things which gratify their flesh, but those who are according to the Spirit and are controlled by the desires of the Spirit set their minds on and seek those things which gratify the (Holy) Spirit. (Ro. 8:5 AMP)

The flesh is weak and vulnerable. Its needs are constant, which puts a strong demand on us to solve the ongoing and immediate issues of life quickly. *Fear* and *Insecurity* put pressure on us to accept the quick fix, "buy now, pay later" solutions offered by the Enemy. The Tempter uses our thinking and feeling and reasoning to try to persuade us to believe, "I can't wait," "I've got to do it myself" and "It is up to me to protect myself in order to stay safe and in control."

Using the mind, will, and emotions (the mind of the flesh) to make the decision will ultimately lead us to choose death. To use a temporary measure to solve a temporary problem that has the eternal consequences of death becomes one of the most effective ways for Satan to propagate his destructive "self-help" policies in the Body of Christ.

> Now the mind of the flesh (which is sense and reason without the Holy Spirit) is death—death that compromises all the miseries arising out of sin both here and hereafter. But the mind of the (Holy) Spirit is life and soul-peace, (freedom from anxiety and emptiness), both now and forever. (Ro. 8:6 AMP)

God wants to bring us back to the place of peace and homeostasis. The only way He can do it is if we trust Him to deal with the *Fear* and *Anxiety* that have become our familiar and constant companions. Their activities are an ever-present part of our environment, the place in which our flesh must operate. Because we are created to live and function out of our divine nature, living contrary to God's nature means we are living in a place of emotional and spiritual emptiness, dissonance and dissatisfaction.

Separation from our divine destiny produces stress and anxiety in us. That separation, also referred to as sin, becomes an open door for the Enemy to come in and plunder our house. God wants to close the gap that separates us from Him, fill the emptiness, and take away the fear and loneliness. Knowing the truth allows Him to heal your heart and take away the pain like no sedative or drug or worldly pursuit ever could. (See *Pain and Suffering* (CD) www.liferecovery.com.)

Self-Reliance: Eating Cookies to Satisfy Our Hunger for God

The Enemy wants to intercept God's message of peace and forgiveness with carnal thoughts that produce self-reliance and put demands on us to try to manage and maintain our own lives. We begin to rely on our biological systems, including our immune system, and our sympathetic nervous system, to provide protection from the onslaught of both spiritual and physical pressures. Our biological systems are not equipped to handle the demonic avalanche generated by *Fear, Stress,* and *Anxiety* that have come to afflict our natural lives on a spiritual level.

Without addressing the spiritual issues at their root, our natural attempts to stop or control them are no more effective than using bonbons to fix a broken heart. Trying to satisfy the hunger for God by eating chocolate chip cookies is not going to work. Filling our soul's emptiness by gratifying our carnal appetites is an *Addiction* waiting to happen. Any system used out of context and not in conformity to the way it is intended to function puts stress on the entire system, opens the door to dysfunction, and brings us into agreement with the lie.

The lie is designed to create a spiritual and systemic opposition to God's original plan and purpose for us that can only be seen as anti-God in its origin. We seldom first recognize any of our problems as spiritual in nature. The anti-God spirit of this world has done an incredible job in blinding the eyes of the unsuspecting and shutting down our ability to discern Satan's counterfeits from God's truth. The disposition of *Hostility* against God that rules the hearts of the hardened and those cut off from the truth prevails in the midst of every decision like the stench of the pig pen, undetected by those who have gotten accustomed to living next to the hog sty.

The spirit of *Stupor* has numbed our senses and closed our eyes to the dangers of the spiritual counterfeits, leaving them either hidden or determined to be nothing of consequence. They are deemed nonexistent and explained away as nothing out of the ordinary until it is too late. We fail to realize that the Earth is under the sway of the Evil One, (Mt. 5:37; 6:13) and influenced by the *Angel of light,* a member of the religious division of *anti-Christ spirits*. Their job is to counterfeit the things of God or slander Him and deceive us, into blaming Him or ourselves, for everything bad that happens to us.

Most often we are quick to join in making an agreement with the *Accuser.* We believe the Devil's version of what happened and charge God with blatant overruling, impatience, impotence, or indifference. All of this works wonderfully in the Enemy's favor as he relentlessly promotes his agenda to call God's motives into question and makes His right to rule the world a matter of opinion. He fills our minds and hearts (our soul) with carnal thoughts and the pursuit of things that are anti-God.

In the midst of this hostility against God, if we refuse to humble ourselves and submit to the counsel of the Spirit of Truth or fail to recognize the need to resist the lies crafted against the truth, we will find ourselves in a place of deception. When we are living in a place of refusing the love of the truth (2 Thess. 2:11), in opposition to the mind of the Spirit (see Ro. 8:7), we are vulnerable to being swept up into error through a passive agreement (Mt. 12:30) made with the Enemy by default.

The choice is ours even though the battle is the Lord's. We find ourselves pulled into the fight, not of our own making, not for the salvation of our souls, but for the enforcement of our freedom. Salvation has given us the freedom to fight, to pursue and to recover the things stolen from us by Satan and regained for us by Christ. Through the victories won at Calvary and enforced by us as part of the army of God on Earth, we have been given the right to take back what has been stolen from us.

Who Directs and Controls You?

"But you are not living the life of the flesh, you are living the life of the Spirit, if the Holy Spirit of God (really) dwells within you—directs and controls you." (Ro. 8:9 AMP). God wants us to give Him control of everything in our lives, including the keeping of our salvation and the sanctification of our souls. (See *Spiritual Foundations* (two-CD set) www.liferecovery.com.)

Permitting God access to every part of us also gives us access to every part of Him. This abiding arrangement is part of the Covenant He made with us through the Cross. It offers us the only way to secure divine protection that insures our eternal and temporal safety. Releasing the control of our lives completely over to the One True God brings us new freedom and liberation from the demonic dictatorship that held us in bondage to doing the things we hated and serving the one who would have destroy us.

Only Christ Jesus can set us free. "Whom the Son sets free is free indeed." John 8:36 remains true in spite of how we feel about it, and even though we are free, we still have the right to choose to walk in that freedom. We are given the option to continue to "live in the flesh—catering to the appetites and impulses of the carnal nature" (Ro. 8:8 AMP), or to "live in the Spirit, directed and controlled by Him." (See Ro. 8:9).

The Bible is clear. "So then those living the life of the flesh, [catering to the appetites and impulses of their carnal nature] cannot please or satisfy God, or be acceptable to Him." (Ro. 8:8 AMP). The Devil knows this and has made it his aim to control our appetites. The control the Enemy intends to exert over us can be best described as programming. If our appetites are being controlled by something outside of us, the question of getting rid of bad habits and sinful behaviors and *Addictions* and losing weight and eating for comfort changes from, "What can I do to stop ...?" to "Who has a hold of me?"

Most of us *never* ask that question. First of all, we fail to understand the need for asking it. Second, we have made the deadly assumption that our appetites are our own. We do not question them as anything that could be coming from anywhere but from our own selves. If I fail to correctly identify the origin of those appetites, trying to control them becomes an act in futility and frustration. I blame myself for not being able to quit, overcome, and stay clean.

Coming into agreement with the assignments *Guilt, Shame, Failure, and Condemnation* are making in my life makes the case for me to take responsibility to quit even more compelling. The idea of free will and "it was my choice" only compound the problem and amplify the need to try harder. If it was my choice, then it is my fault. "I should have, could have, and need to" all distract me from asking the right questions. Was it my choice or have I been coerced by *Cravings* or conditioned by *Fear* or controlled by the need to have *Control?* What has brought me to this miserable state of bondage? I am consumed with either assigning or assuming blame, on the one hand, while obsessed with trying to stop doing the thing I hate, on the other.

Who Will Deliver Me?

Paul realized his dilemma was a matter beyond will-power and self-control. The struggle had gotten out of hand and had taken a hold of his members. He was being strangled by the thing that was warring inside of him. His only defense was the simple cry, "O wretched man that I am, who will deliver me from this body of death?" Who will have mercy on me and set me free from this demonic programming, this "software from hell" that *Addiction* and *Craving* have set up inside of me?

He knew it was not a matter of diet and discipline. It was a matter of deliverance. The demonic spirit needed to be removed, not reformed or reincorporated into a do-it-yourself spirituality emerging out of a greater self-awareness and touted to be the latest, greatest break-through revelation in some mystic meditation or self-ascending, self-help madness.

"Is it me?" is the first question that begs the second. Could there be other things operating in my life that are not me, things I may not be aware of that are defeating both my personal and spiritual efforts to recover my life and be restored to health? The short answer is yes. The long answer is too many to count. Let us begin by considering the electrical and biochemical basics of biological functioning in our internal communication system and what could go wrong or be manipulated neurologically to make us more vulnerable to the attack of the Enemy.

- It is hard to see what I do not want to see. What is it that you do not want to look at in your life?
- Is it possible that there is something in me that is controlling me and keeping me doing the thing I do not want to do?
- Could it be that I am being held hostage in my own soul?

Chapter 12

Take Down the Tower

The main control tower for the routing of incoming information (the stimuli picked up by the radar operating through the five senses) is the hypothalamus. Through the body's communication systems, the hypothalamus is linked to every command site in the body including the nervous system and the endocrine system (glands). The Hypothalamus sits as the interpretive center of the brain, screening and interpreting both the messages that are coming into the brain and those being sent from the brain to the various organs of the body. It also monitors the messages being sent throughout the body from one organ to another and back to the brain.

The work of the hypothalamus makes that which is intangible tangible and brings the inertia of an idea (thought) into motion and gives it a concrete design. The hypothalamus assesses the critical importance of the information being sent from our external and internal world and sends a corresponding response. It is the place where perceptions are formed that allows us to interact with the spiritual and the natural worlds. The place where the spiritual and natural worlds intersect makes the hypothalamus both a critical and strategic objective for the Enemy in his battle to capture us.

It is like the mechanical room of a building. To expedite our takeover, the Enemy must control the hypothalamus. If he can transmit wrong information to the unsuspecting receivers or cause incoming stimuli to be misinterpreted, he can control our actions and reactions. Because all parts of the brain, including the hypothalamus, play a critical part in the health and homeostasis of the body, it must be captured in order for the Enemy's body of death soul-software to operate effectively.

By controlling the "control tower," the demonic reprogramming of both the soul (the mind, will, and emotions) and the body can be accomplished by simply interfering with the electrical and chemical messages that the hypothalamus is trying to interpret and send through the communications systems. Not only are the messages often demonically interrupted and inspired, the body itself becomes the battlefield for much of the rest of what goes on in this spiritual war, with the organs becoming prime targets in the attack. (See *A Case for Healing* (Manual) and *Spiritual Root Causes of Physical Diseases* (CD) www.liferecovery.com.)

One of the most strategic and critical components in the defense system and a strong determinate in the outcome of any war is maintaining the integrity of the communications systems that link the members of the body together. Targeting the communication systems in order to control the information being sent through the body becomes another one of Satan's most effective schemes in destroying the human body and the soul of the one who dwells in it.

The Body of Death programming software used by the Enemy to control our biological system evidently operates through frequency manipulation and impulse control. If all human-life functions at their basic level are neurological impulses (frequencies), and if those impulses are counterfeited or intercepted or the neuro-pathways those messages must travel on are frayed, broken, or controlled by the Enemy, the health and productivity of that individual is greatly compromised, if not completely halted.

In a natural take-down there are any number of ways power lines can be tampered with or affected in the physical world. The lines can be cut, short-circuited, over stimulated, or intercepted. Our spiritual Enemy uses similar strategies to execute the capture and takedown of our body's electrical circuits. The more successful he is in interfering with our communication/defense systems without arousing our suspicions, the more useful his "bot" systems will be in establishing his ultimate control over us. The "bot", short for "robot", is a program that is running in the background doing things we are not aware of. In the computer world they can be beneficial or maleficent.

"Bot" is derived from the word "robot" and is an automated process that interacts with other network services. A malicious bot is self-propagating malware designed to infect a host. Bots rarely announce their presence with high scan rates, which damage network infrastructure; instead they infect networks in a way that escapes immediate notice.

http://www.cisco.com/web/about/security/intelligence/virus-worm-diffs.html

Lies and Lines

Life is vulnerable to attack and capture in any number of ways. Interference at any point within any part of any one of its systems creates a breach in the internal security within the whole. Tampering with the neurological frequencies or chemical equations or the circuits on which they travel is strategic in tipping the delicate balance of the body's biological and psychological systems.

If the accuracy and speed with which the neurological messages reaching their destination are essential to the health and functioning of the body in both ordinary and extreme situations, then both the messages and the communication lines over which they are sent are vulnerable and must be protected if we are to win the war on sickness and slavery. The communication network links our spiritual, mental, emotional, and biological systems to provide a grid through which life-energy and information travels to and through the body.

How Does the Central Nervous System Work?

The body relies on two different systems for the dissemination of the gathered information, the nervous system, which uses neurological impulses transmitted as frequencies, and the glandular system, which operates through chemical messaging. The two create within the body a sort of a chemical-electromagnetic communication grid that sustains our life by linking all parts of our body together with neurological impulses. These impulses connect not only the organs, but also the whole body with the parts of the brain that respond to the mind, emotions, and will.

Waves of physical and chemical excitation that carry messages along a nerve fiber in response to a stimulus are called neurological impulses. These waves of excitation causes a change in the electrical charge in the cell or membrane of the nerve fiber. All of the cells in our body form organs that are connected into systems that work in conjunction with each other. None of those systems are capable of working in isolation without interdependence upon the others.

The nervous system controls and coordinates the functioning of all other systems in response to our surroundings. Each stimulus or change in our environment is detected by our senses and sent as neurological messages to the brain. They are interpreted by the brain, which then sends directions to the various organs and extremities of the body to respond and adapt to conditions as those situations might affect our body and our safety.

The function of the neurological system is to transmit and receive a constant series of messages via electrical impulses to and from the control center situated in the brain. The nervous system is divided into the central nervous system (CNS) that includes the brain and spinal cord, and the peripheral nervous system (PNS), comprising cranial nerves and spinal nerves.

The PNS includes nerves emerging from the brain (cranial nerves) and nerves emerging from the spinal cord (spinal nerves). These nerves are divided into sensory nerves that conduct messages from various parts of the body to the CNS, and motor nerves that conduct impulses from the CNS to muscles and glands. The PNS is further divided into the Somatic Nervous System (SNS) and Autonomic Nervous System (ANS),.

The SNS consists of sensory neurons from the head, body wall, extremities, and motor neurons to skeletal muscle. These motor responses are under conscious control, and therefore the SNS is voluntary. Other peripheral nerves perform specialized functions and form the autonomic nervous system, (ANS); they control various activities that occur automatically or involuntarily such as the contraction of smooth muscle in the walls of the digestive system. The autonomic system is further divided into the sympathetic and parasympathetic systems. These two systems provide nerve stimuli to the same organs throughout the body, but bring about different effects.

The sympathetic nervous system helps prepare the body for "fight or flight" and creates conditions in the tissues for physical activity. It is stimulated by strong emotions, such as anger and excitement, and will therefore speed up the heart rate, increase the activity of sweat glands and the adrenals, and decrease those of the digestive system. It also produces rapid redistribution of blood between the skin and skeletal muscles.

Conversely, the parasympathetic nervous system slows down the body and helps prepare for a more relaxed state, ready for digestion and sleep. It will therefore increase peristalsis of the alimentary canal, slow down the heart rate, and constrict the bronchioles in the lungs. The balance between these two systems is controlled to create a state of homeostasis. This is where the internal stability of the bodily systems is maintained in response to the external environment.

The CSN creates a communication network which serves as the pathways over which the neurological impulses travel. The brain, heart, and every organ of the body generate signals that are actually electrical charges that create a stream of electrical current that travels along the nerve fibers.

The information is carried in the form of slight changes in the electrical charges in the nerve fibers. The central nervous system, with its different subsystems, provides the body with instantaneous and current status reports that keep the entire body fully informed. These subtle electromagnetic current changes allow the body to respond to the slightest change in the environment or the emotions of the person.

Frequencies

Frequencies play a critical role in the takeover of the human being. If everything at its most basic level of functioning can be described and identified as a specific frequency, then the most basic level at which control must be achieved is at the level of frequencies and neurological impulses. The Enemy knows that if he can interfere with or manipulate our biological systems at the core level of electrical impulses and frequencies by simply altering the food we eat or interfering with our neurological systems, he can control us at every level.

The electrical pulses that carry the messages vibrate at different frequencies. In fact, every organ of the body vibrates at a different frequency, which allows the recipient of the message to specifically identify the source of the message that is being sent to the brain. Not only does the body identify its various members through frequencies, it also communicates with itself within a certain range of frequencies.

Frequencies are measured in megahertz with the body's optimal health ranging from between 62–68 MHz in the daytime. There has been a great deal of research in the area of measuring frequencies in the last two decades to determine their effects on the health of the body. Some of those findings have brought to light the importance of maintaining the body's frequency levels within the 62–68 MHz range for good health. When the frequency levels drop, the immune system is compromised. The more it falls, the more susceptible the person becomes to serious physical diseases. Some of the scientific pioneers in the study of frequencies are included in the references below.

http://justalist.blogspot.com/2008/03/vibrational-frequency-list.html

cellphonesafety.wordpress.com/2006/09/17/ the-frequency-of-the-human-bodyand-your-coffee/

Because everything has frequencies, gaining control of the thing that controls our frequencies, including food or chemical substances, for example, gives the one who wants to control the frequencies a great advantage in being able to control everything. Remember, food has frequencies. Controlling the foods we eat and the quality of that food gives the Enemy an incredible advantage in taking over our spiritual effectiveness as well as our bodily health. Drugs also have frequencies. Many of the foods and drinks and drugs we ingest are "dead." Their frequency levels are not high enough to keep us in the optimum "megahertz frequency levels" to keep our immune systems strong.

Chapter 13

The Food Fight from Hell

For those of us who submit to the "God-is-the-Creator" version of what happened in the beginning, we know that God created life-giving management systems and placed them within our bodies for the sole purpose of preserving and maintaining the functioning of our bodies. One of those systems is the hunger-satiation system designed to detect when nutrients are in short supply in the body.

Natural biochemical cravings signal for more of what is needed in the body to maintain healthy functioning. The hunger-satiation system conducts a legitimate function for the body in providing essential minerals and nutrients for sustaining and protecting the proper operation of its life-support systems. But what if that natural craving mechanism itself has come under the control of the Enemy? What if what I am craving is something that is not good for me?

What if our cravings for sweets and carbs and cigarettes and certain junk foods and alcohol are simply counterfeit activities being conducted on a legal highway? What if the body is not able to discern the regular, God-given cravings that are now being used by the Enemy because they are couched in familiar groupings and not identified as anything different than the normal, legitimate requests made by the body for its daily ration of food and water? Could this intense craving for sugar be coming out of a mineral deficiency, or even a unidentified hunger for God, and if it is, how will those needs be satisfied by eating another donut?

Breaking It All Down into Bite-Sized Pieces

Something that is essential for the continuance of life would be classified as vital. If we break life down into its smallest bits of matter, we discover atoms and molecules. Those bits of matter are in constant motion. We call that motion *energy*. Energy gives life and motion to the matter or material substance of our body. Energy can also be described in terms of small rapid movements called vibrations. Vibrations are patterns of movement. They move at certain predetermined rates called frequencies. Frequencies identify locations and send messages.

Everything emits frequencies. Bananas have a frequency. The color yellow has a different frequency than the color green. In the human body, some believe that the different organs transmit different frequencies that are used to send specific messages to other parts of the body. The frequency of the liver sends a message to the heart. The heart is able to identify both the message and where the message is coming from because the specific frequencies of all the various members of the body are known to each other. Otherwise, what would happen if the members of our body could not "talk" to each other or be able to communicate their present status and needs with one another?

*https://cellphonesafety.wordpress.com/2006/09/17/
the-frequency-of-the-human-bodyand-your-coffee/*

*http://ezinearticles.
com/?Electromagnetic-Charges-in-Food!&id=1421536*

Each object has its own distinct frequency and thus can be identified by its frequency much like every radio station has its own designated signal or frequency. We can tune into a specific radio station by tuning into its frequency. We search for the specific radio station that carries the sound waves for our favorite songs and announcements. Those songs and sounds are carried from one radio tower or transmitter to another until it reaches our receptor site, in this case, our radio device. The frequencies are sent through our listening device and picked up by our ears. Our hypothalamus operates like a receptor site. It receives the information and sends it to our understanding where it is interpreted and decoded to mean something.

Frequencies carry information as vibrations. Those vibrations carry the information along pathways much like electric circuits transfer electricity to the various rooms of your house. The body stays connected with itself through various systems of circuitry. Each of these connective systems allows the conduction of frequencies along our neurological pathways that relay information and energy to every member of the body to maintain the life activities of the body. This system generally known as our nervous system has several subsystems. They are strung together like an electrical circuit to form the communication lines that link the organs of the body together. The neurological vibrations or frequencies travel as nerve impulses through the neurons circuits carrying the messages and commands to the various places throughout the body.

All of the neurological messages sent through the body are carried as electromagnetic charges called frequencies. Life is made up of a continuous stream of neurological impulses. Without the continuous stream of neurological impulses flowing through our bodies, we are dead! Any restriction of the neurological impulses or their passage or the alteration of their route will affect the functioning of the entire system.

The body begins to deteriorate any place where those neurological impulses are pinched off or subluxated. Poor posture, degenerated discs, and inadequate nutrition interfere with the pathways on which those messages travel. Breaking off neuro-pathways or hindering nerve impulses creates friction, irritation, and overheating, which promotes generalized anxiety and system fatigue. Interference along these neurological pathways, therefore, becomes an important strategy in the Enemy's plot to destroy us.

Life in Its Smallest Bits

A second communication system, known as the endocrine system is a glandular system, which sends chemical messages through the body in a somewhat similar fashion as the neurological system only it uses chemicals instead of electrical impulses. The chemicals used in this system are called hormones. In the nervous system electrical messages move along the neurons to the dendrites, (the finger-like endings of a nerve) to the synapse where they are turned into a chemical message, using the neurotransmitters as a sort of chemical alphabet to carry these chemical message across the synapses (tiny chemical bodies of fluid). On the other side of the synapse they are reconnect with dendrites where they turn back into electrical messages. The dendrites are connected to other neurons that carry the electrical impulse along the nerve pathway (neuron) thus carrying the message to the next synapse where the process is repeated again until the message gets to its final destination.

The communication process for both systems begins with incoming stimuli gathered through the five senses which are decoded and interpreted by the hypothalamus. The information is then sent as a chemical or electrical message through the endocrine (glandular) or nervous systems to its intended receiver. Messages can also be sent from the mind, will and emotions (soul) or from the individual organs back to the brain, making the communications systems act like a two-way highway.

"Feeling like a bundle of nerves" is more than just a saying. Fear stimulates an increase in the release of nervous energy. Excessive nervous energy creates anxiety that mixes with the original message or misfires a neurological impulse of its own. The overexcitation of the system often caused by the increased demand to do something while simultaneously, not knowing what to do causes the system to overheat.

Fear and *Confusion* create friction and stress in the body, like driving 80 mph with the brakes on. The release of too much electrical energy into the nervous system with the simultaneous resistance creates irritation and agitation, which can overload a circuit and make you feel like you are going crazy or losing it. If the overload is too great, there will be a blackout like when an electrical circuit is overloaded.

Nerve impulses carry the messages coded as subtle changes in electrical activity from the brain down the spinal cord to be disbursed throughout the nervous system. Much of this process is done without our conscious awareness as the information runs through the autonomic nervous system, which does not require our understanding or direct input to function. Many of these activities include things like the heart rate, breathing, metabolism, balance, and the digestion of our food.

The automatic maintenance of the body's routine life-support functions is rooted in subconscious physiological and psychological reactions. Our brain and body are responding to stimuli at an unconscious level rather than as a specific rational conscious response we would make to a situation if our mind were involved at a level of thinking. This frees us up to do the more fun things in life without having to worry about remembering to breathe and digest our food.

Because so many of these chemical and neurological processes are out of our hands, it would be difficult to imagine having to manage or try to fix or adjust them through willpower or self-control. These functions operate outside of the area of conscious thought and therefore do not readily respond to conscious directives.

One of the main parts of the process that does require our approval and conscious cooperation, however, is in choosing the foods or chemicals we ingest into our bodies. We often make those selections based on cravings, convenience, and taste rather than nutritional needs. From the selections we are making, our body must try to find whatever it needs to build and maintain our physical strength. We must live in this house our entire life. The condition of our house depends upon the foods we are willing to provide for it. How nice of a house would you live in if you built it using rotten lumber and rusty nails?

The Grid

Through the operating privileges the Serpent, a.k.a. Satan, obtained in the Garden, he has been permitted to download the spirit of death operating software into the body via the soul. Paul describes this programming as "the body of sin" (Ro. 6:6) and the "body of death" (Ro. 7:24).

Our beliefs systems are formed out of our past experiences and our perception of them. These beliefs form the grid through which new incoming stimuli must pass and from which future decisions are made. If much of the information contained in that grid has been skewed or is incorrect, what are the chances that a new or correct response will be made to any new situations using old information? Believing the lies to be the truth permits error to continue to operate as truth in us.

Believing the accuracy of our own personal experiences only perpetuates a system that is broken. Because those beliefs are already so familiar to us, however, they often never get re-evaluated or changed or challenged. The stimuli coming into our minds are filtered through this grid of lies which then influences the commands and decisions sent by the mind to the body. If the information has been processed through a belief system that is based on past perceptions that are not correct, it sends out a message of fear.

Because all of our biological systems operate on the level of frequencies and filters that color and interpret our perceptions of our experiences, interference with either the filters or the frequencies that control us is one of the Devil's most effective ways to mess up our entire system, both physically and spiritually. All he has to do is alter the frequencies or corrupt the filters through which we see things and he has captured us. This takes the battle for freedom and the recovery from an addiction out of our hands. The typical willpower, self-help methods will not work, and we find ourselves catapulted into a whole new arena of spiritual warfare that takes prisoners at the level of subconscious thought and physical manipulation.

So What?

Programming uses a specific set of information or operational codes to control a vessel. When the Enemy psychologically reconditions us, he is attempting to re-code or override the initial, divine operating codes in order to control the function of the vessel. He disrupts signals and twists the incoming information through the perception grid and redirects it through the new codes and triggers he has imbedded into us. He uses these to guide and manipulate our mind and body into doing what he wants. Using the lies we have come into agreement with to authorize a new set of predetermined commands, the Enemy uses cravings and coercion to set up and control the operation of various members of our physical bodies.

For example, the Divine command God gave to my immune system was to protect and preserve my life. If, however, through my experiences in the pit of life I have come to believe I am bad, my agreement with the lie sends a new set of commands to my immune system. Because each of us has been authorized to speak on our own, our immune system becomes confused with the two contradicting commands. It now sees me as both good and bad. If I am seen as the enemy, my immune system is prompted to take action against me. This compromising of my immune system can trigger any number of immune system diseases and disorders in my body.

So what do frequencies and coding and programming and nerve impulses have to do with addictions or eating food or controlling cravings or going on diets or doing the will of God? The answer is everything! At its basic level, we are what we eat. We must eat to live. If that is true, then in some undeniable way, what we eat forms the basic core of our health and how we feel. This makes our food a very strategic part of the battle for our souls.

Like everything else, food has frequencies. If the frequencies in the food are altered or dead, they will deplete or interfere with or change the strength of the original frequencies that are needed to run the body's operating systems at optimum levels of health. If the Enemy can entice us to eat dead food or drink toxic liquids, he can lower the body's energy levels and reprogram it for sickness and death.

The food God gave us was meant to nourish the body and supply it with the raw materials that could be converted into energy to replenish depleted cells and rebuild new ones. Calories, (a unit of energy-producing potential in food) are like the BTUs that come from converting the raw materials: proteins, carbohydrates, and fats into usable bits of energy. The food is metabolized or broken down into its elemental form to provide the energy and the living material the body needs to make amino acids, enzymes, blood, bones, and plasma to stay alive.

The Enemy's plan is simple. If he can change, interfere with, or control our eating habits, he can change, interfere with, and control those things that govern the life and health of our body at the cellular level. Our agreement with his plan allows him to ultimately control our frequencies and destroy our souls through something as simple as the food we choose to eat or not eat.

Blackouts

The quality of our life, including our health and safety, is dependent upon the quality of food as much as the quantity. The life-giving nutrients, vitamins, and minerals not only provide the building blocks for the maintenance of the body and its frequencies but also feed the systems through which those nutrients are sent. God designed the food He created to provide the right frequencies for the body to repair and heal itself.

We know that every atom is made up of protons and electrons, which give the body a slight electrical charge.

The body is made up of about 70 percent water. Water is a great conductor of electricity. As with any electrical circuit, there are certain minerals and elements such as copper, , that are used to increase conductivity in the wires. So, too, the nerves in the body require similar minerals to enhance their conductivity for the electrical currents that travel as neurological impulses through them.

To keep the body's circuits running at optimum levels the right minerals and organic building materials are vital. Just as defective or overloaded circuits can cause the electrical system to short out, blackouts and shutdowns will decrease or cut off the supply of energy necessary for the neurological functioning and health of the body. When there is a cessation of the neurological impulses, the body dies.

The fascinating difference between the wiring in your house and the nerves in your body is that the body is an organic, living organism that has been programmed by God to know how to repair itself. Self-repair is only found in living systems, not those made by man. The only problem with the self-regenerating system given to rebuild the body is its vulnerability to the quality of the food that is necessary for those repairs to be done well. Health and feeling good are directly related to choosing to give our body the healthy food it needs to live.

Indulgent and rebellious eating hinders our life processes in every way. If not eating right causes the health of our bodies to be undermined, and we are built to want to live, why would anyone in their right mind willingly participate in a plan to destroy their own body? Could it be that the "internal emergencies" created by Craving's demands for an immediate solution pressure us into make a hasty choice and get a quick fix right now?

When the body is under too much stress the demand for problem solving and data processing increases. This has a negative effect on productivity. The increased pressure drains our energy. Our ability to deal with the flood of too much stimuli flowing through our nervous system all at once overloads the circuits. We are stuck trying to solve the irresolvable conflicts of life, and we crash.

This puts pressure on our emotional and physical equilibrium that causes us to feel irritable or panicky or anxious. The body cannot sustain the energy levels required to live in this kind of fight–flight state indefinitely. The feelings of an internal emergency create chaos in the systems, which actually decrease our ability to think clearly. We instinctively look for ways to relieve the stress that would allow the body to go back into a more natural resting state. The crisis of physical and emotional problems makes us vulnerable to the counterfeit solutions of pills, junk food, and chemicals, which includes both legal and illegal drugs.

To Summarize

Food has frequencies. God's food has the frequencies necessary to maintain health at the cellular level. Dead food cannot provide the body with the living material it needs to grow, think, or execute the many daily functions necessary to keep it flushed and flourishing. The biological harmony of our physical and mental health is determined, at least in part, by the quality of the food we eat, which makes our spiritual resistance to the spirits of

Cravings and *Addiction* contingent upon our willingness to eat the foods God has provided.

- Have you ever felt like a bundle of nerves?
- Are you picky or pleased with what He has provided for you to eat?
- What keeps you from eating some of the foods you don't like?
- Food is more powerful than we think. How does your relationship with food affect your relationship with yourself? Your body image?
- What are some of your favorite weaknesses when it comes to food?

Mini-Glossary – a Summary of Common Words

Vital — crucial to the survival or continuing effectiveness of something, needed for life, required for the continuance of life.

Vibrations — small rapid movements, to shake, whip, or weave.

Frequency — the fact of something happening often or regularly at short intervals, rate of occurrence, number of times something happens during a particular period of time. Frequency is the number of occurrences of a repeating event per unit time. It could also be referred to as temporal frequency. The period is the duration of one cycle in a repeating event, so the period is the reciprocal of the frequency.

Nerve — bundle of fibers forming a network that transmits messages in the form of impulses between the brain or spinal cord and the body's organs.

Nervousness — state of emotional agitation.

Nervous—feeling of dread or apprehension, inability to tolerate anxiety and stress.

Nerve impulse—a rapid and momentary change in electrical activity that passes along a nerve fiber to other neurons, muscles, or other body organs and signals instructions or information.

Nerve center—control center: a place from which a large organization, system, or network of nerves is controlled.

Program—instructions obeyed by computer, operating instructions for a machine, a set of coded operating instructions that is used to run a machine automatically, to insert coded operating instructions into a machine.

Nutrients—any substance that provides nourishment; the minerals the plants take from the soil converted into edible form to keep the body healthy and help it grow.

Chapter 14

Conditioning and Counterfeits

Looking more closely at the power of programming we might ask, "Is there a link between natural cravings and those out-of-control demands that begin to reshape our lives around a substance? How can something as natural as bodily appetites be connected with something as psychological as an addiction?" Without minimizing the situation or overspiritualizing things, let us take a look at the biological systems and their function or dysfunction to see if they could create in us any psychological or spiritual vulnerabilities.

One of the Enemy's favorite schemes for concealing the true spiritual nature of the battle with *Addictions* and *Cravings* is to hide his activity in the business of life. If he can get us busy looking in the wrong direction for a solution, we will start doing, denying, and dieting to try to deal with the problems *Addiction* sets up. Doing, denying and dieting all operate out of our natural inclination to manage a negative situation or solve a problem or prove we are right or feel better or try to survive. Before we realize it, we are caught up in trying to quit the thing we cannot stop, until doing and stopping all run together in some crazy out-of-control cycle.

The BOT

The Enemy takes advantage of our predispositions and desires to overcome an undesirable behavior like an addiction, for example, by offering a counterfeit solution. Once the Enemy gets us to agree with his solution, he can set up his pseudo-operating program within us. This counterfeit craving software, for example, overrides the natural systems by acting like a "bot" within the system.

A bot is a program that is hidden within a legitimate operating program that runs its illegal hidden agenda off the energy of the legitimate system in order to disable the functioning and integrity of the original operating system. What is true in the world of computers serves as a good analogy for what is happening in our own bodies. The Bible tells us to beware of the *Antichrist spirits* who come in the guise of Christ to destroy the work of Christ. This is very similar to what a bot does; coming in guised as part of our legitimate physical and psychological operating system it seeks to destroy us.

The Conditioning

Here is the general method of reconditioning the Enemy uses to establish demonic control of our bodies. First, he must get us to agree with his lies. The Devil uses our God-given legitimate systems of hunger and learning, for example, to convince us to believe something other than what God says is true, to be true or helpful. God has given us a sense of hunger to help us know when the body requires fuel and we need to eat. Those feelings are designed by God and wired into us at a subconscious level as an impulse to cause us to want to eat food when the body needs it.

Our learning system "fires and wires" things together, causing us to remember what we learned for future reference. The Enemy uses our learning system to "wire" his lie together with something that is already identified as good or true. For example, love, which is something good and necessary, is wired with sexual abuse by causing the love and abuse to "fire" together simultaneously. Abuse is now perceived to be an act of love especially if accompanied by other reinforcing data also perceived to be part of love like a soft, non-threatening tone of voice. Wiring the two together equates the lie with the truth and elevates the position of the lie to the place of truth.

This new "equation" is a lie that now gets to operate like the truth in our body. Believing the lie that "I like the taste of sugar; therefore sugar is good," for example, gives the lie that "Sugar is good and desirable," the power to act as truth in our belief system. The "new truth" is then written into our processing systems and included with the other personal data we have collected from our past experiences, giving it the same operating privileges established by God in the original software. Those operating privileges work as a power of suggestion to change and influence any future decisions we make, in this case, about eating sugar, and includes those choices that are made at the subconscious level of functioning.

The new information is generalized to include other similar situations and as a result, our desire for sweets expands to include other things that turn to sugar in our system, like alcohol. Having experienced the quick and immediate boost sugar gives to our energy levels reinforces the behavior and becomes the hook that conditions us to reach for it the next time we are feeling down or tired.

The Enemy can also target our emotions by firing together the comfort that comes from satisfying our physical hunger with the need to find comfort from emotional pain. An empty stomach is equated with feelings of pain and discomfort. Pain is also a common condition of the heart. Food is now perceived as a means to fill both an empty stomach and an empty heart. Firing them together wires them together. A new equation is written in our experiences and stored in our memory. Food is now seen as a solution to fixing our emotional discomfort.

When natural hunger is wired to emotional pain the crossover creates confusion in the system as food or drink or chemical substances (though not the legitimate remedy for emotional pain) become the newly conditioned responses to dealing with emotional pain. The mind begins to make the assumption that every time the body is feeling emotion pain, it is a call for food. And when we feel a legitimate hunger for food, emotional pain is tied in with it. This gives emotional pain the same power to stimulate a call for food as natural hunger. The person begins to eat for comfort. Thus, whenever there is a natural physical hunger, there is also a constant danger and demand for the body to eat to fill an emotional vacuum, as well.

This creates a problem we call emotional eating that is becoming a habit. We are now conditioned to eat or drink or use substances when we are sad, lonely, or anxious because we have now been conditioned to believe food and alcohol or the drug of choice will ease the pain, be it natural hunger or emotional emptiness. Every time the system is stimulated with either genuine hunger or the newly conditioned stimulus (emotional pain), we want food or drink or drugs. The more intense the pain is, the more urgent the demand to ease that pain.

Part of the reason it is so hard to break the habit in any particular *Addiction* is because it is hard for us to distinguish between what is the genuine need for food or relief from pain and the lie that the body has been trained or conditioned to do to respond to that need. The spirit of *Cravings* has written a new script into our body's operating software and tampered with the information grid.

Food and eating are intensified and generalized to become the response to more and more circumstances. The Enemy has successfully created a new set of stimuli that are able to pull up the eating response. That eating response can also be generalized to call for the ingesting of things other than food. As the number of substances that can be substituted for food grows, the Enemy can replace food with alcohol, drugs, and prescription drugs, to satisfy emotional pain. *Cravings* has unlocked the system through conditioning and is now able to mingle his preferred responses as the solution to a growing number of physical and psychological feelings and needs.

The Spirit of Cravings

The *spirit of Cravings* now takes the natural impulse to eat and the newly conditioned stimuli (emotional pain) that has been wired to it and charges them with the power to create an urgency to eat or drink or ingest chemicals that have been programmed in as solutions to the pain. That compelling urge or lust demands action and allows *Cravings* to take control of the person's will. It sets up a demand for a substance, including junk food or drugs, to calm the system. *Cravings* is manipulating the situations to use food and drugs in ways they were never intended to be used to resolve psychological and spiritual needs in a way God never intended them to be used. The Enemy now uses the genuine spiritual hunger created by God to stimulate us to take in nourishment to satisfy the body and dull the spiritual appetite. He uses fear and pain and feelings of emptiness as a trigger to get us to eat bad food or do drugs in order to feel better, take away the pain, fill the emptiness, and calm our anxiety without putting God into the equation.

Because the "bot" is connected to an authorized system and because we do still have legitimate needs to eat food, the counterfeit system is both hard to detect or separate from the authentic operating system. This makes it hard to identify, expose, or break. You might be wondering what all of this has to do with losing weight or getting free from drugs or smoking or staying sober. A better question would be, "How do diets and drug programs deal with bots and the demonic intelligence behind them?"

Pressure to Act

Chemical and neurological depletion of the physical systems also creates an internal pressure inside of us that calls for action. The urgency of that call weakens our resistance and causes us to give into *Cravings*. Natural hunger pangs that signal the body to eat and drink are normal. The *spirit of Cravings* is not natural or normal. It triggers a stronger, more out-of-control demand for certain foods or substances that we have been conditioned to believe will alleviate the pain or relieve the pressure.

Physiologically, natural cravings can sometimes come in response to a lack of minerals or nutrients that disrupt the equilibrium and balance that are necessary to maintain a sense of wellbeing in the body. Many times we are compelled by racing thoughts and a panic response to re-establish our chemical balances to calm the out-of-control feelings we are experiencing. We will reach for whatever we have been conditioned to believe will work to manipulate our feelings to bring us back within the range of feeling good. Some have been conditioned to respond to that anxiety by using food inappropriately or drugs.

We can also eat and drink and use in an effort to compensate for something we sense is missing. Meaninglessness and a life without purpose are prime targets for this kind of carnal attempt to fill the emptiness or boredom of our souls with what some, call, "mindless eating." We have been conditioned through the use of food to believe that putting things into our mouths will fill the vacuum of our souls and bring comfort.

The feelings of discomfort can come out of both physical hunger and emotional feelings of abandonment and past hurts. Consequently, putting something into our mouth becomes a powerful response to discomfort. We have learned even in infancy that bottles and pacifiers can be substituted for nursing which naturally brings comfort. Consequently, because we learned as infants that putting something into our mouths brought comfort; bottles and things held by the mouth became identified as triggers for comfort. Because the original experiences were deemed to be genuine, we have learned (been conditioned) to automatically apply the old solutions to new situations that seem to be similar, believing they will still be able to bring us comfort in the new situation.

The connection between the memory of the old trigger, (the bottle) and the current experience, (pain) moves along a pathway created in the original learning event. This makes it possible for the old, learned information stored in the brain to be revived (remembered). An electrical signal is sent along the already-existing neurological pathway to generate a similar response to the new situation, which now calls for putting something into the mouth, (food, cigarettes, snuff, gum, candy, cans of soda or bottles of beer, etc.).

If those electrical and chemical triggers and the neuro-pathways they use are the result of demonic conditioning, (things we learned through our experiences in the "Snake Pit"), we may not realize it, but we have been rewired by the Enemy. This gives him control over our actions, causing us to "do the things we do not want to do" that the Apostle Paul talks about. The results will be manifested in us and through us as *Addictions* and *Cravings* and their first cousins, *Obsessions* and *Compulsions*.

They all seem to create the same compelling pressures in us to act in a certain way by demanding certain responses to emotional or chemical disturbance in the brain or body. Whether those demands are real or perceived to be real, we feel compelled to act upon them. The pressure to act creates an obsession with an idea or a feeling, which calls for a specific response. The misfiring of information (fear) in the orbital cortex signals the call for a prescribed response to the problem. If the misfiring is persistent and the problem is unaffected, the incessant demands force the signals to repeat, creating compulsions. These compulsions are triggered by *Fear* and *Failure*. The correct biological or psychological response to the problem have been replaced by a specific patterned response to a set of information that has deliberately been tampered with to cause the orbital cortex to classifying things as dangerous that are not. This causes an incorrect identification of both the problem and what needs to be done to fix it.

OCD and the Brain—Andrew B. Hollander

Obsessive Compulsive Disorder (OCD), as defined by Andrew B. Hollander, identifies several key features including the preoccupation with disturbing thoughts that our minds feel compelled to address.

Obsessions are unwanted ideas, disturbing thoughts, or impulses such as fear of contamination from germs, or fear that one might accidentally harm a loved one."

Hollander continues.

"These obsessions often produce great anxiety. To deal with this overwhelming anxiety, a person with OCD often resorts to repetitive behaviors called compulsions. Some of the most common compulsions are washing, checking, hoarding, and repeating (1). The compulsions are often mental problems such as list making, counting, or repeating words or phrases (2). These obsessions and compulsions make up the OCD cycle.

The person has obsessions that cause anxiety. To alleviate the anxiety, the person acts out the compulsions. The rituals provide temporary relief but often the symptoms worsen (1). People with OCD often recognize the irrationality of their obsessions and compulsions and they do not derive pleasure from their rituals. Because of their understanding of the senselessness of their actions, people with OCD often try to suppress their thoughts or resist compulsive behavior (2). However, over time the anxiety is often too much to handle and the symptoms are ultimately manifested, sometimes to the point that the rituals are so time consuming that the person is not able to function."

"Researchers hypothesize that the orbital cortex alerts the brain to a problem and that in OCD it sends out repeated false alarms. Those signals go to the caudate nucleus, which is involved in controlling the movement of the limbs."(8)

Hollander cites the work of Schwartz, another researcher who explains that the "orbital cortex is like a warning light [and] it's the job of the caudate nucleus to switch that warning light off." (8) The alarm signal spreads from the caudate nucleus to the cingulated gyrus. Normally, "high level thought processes override the distress signals and cause the caudate nucleus to switch them off." (8) However, in OCD this does not happen. From the PET scans, Schwartz found that the regions metabolize the glucose quickly, in "correlated rates—as if they were interlocked."(8) "All four structures seem to be madly interlocking in OCD patients: the orbital cortex fires frantic messages to the caudate nucleus, which simultaneously receives signals of fear erroneously stirred up by the cingulated gyrus. As a result, a person tries some form of corrective behavior, but the 'warning light' stays on." (8) In other words, the caudate nucleus "is like a gate that is stuck open so that impulses which are normally locked out are let through... [thus] the perceptions of something wrong keep coming in."

The circuit is completed by the cingulated gyrus, the "gear shifter" of the mind. Increased activity in the anterior cingulated gyrus and prefrontal cortex is often associated with problems shifting attention which may be clinically manifested by cognitive inflexibility, obsessive thoughts, compulsive behaviors, excessive worrying, argumentativeness, oppositional behavior or "getting stuck" on certain thoughts or actions. We have seen a strong association with this finding and obsessive-compulsive disorders, oppositional defiant disorders, eating disorders, addictive disorders, anxiety disorders, Tourette's syndrome and chronic pain (especially when combined with increased basal ganglia activity).

-Article printed from Amen Clinics: http://www.amen-clinics.com OCD and the Brain—Andrew B. Hollander

http://serendip.brynmawr.edu/bb/neuro/neur000/web1/Hollander.html

Chapter 15

The Template of Spiritual Warfare

If we overlay the template of spiritual warfare on top of this rather sophisticated scientific description of the body's biological information processing center, we can see multiple ways for the Enemy to sabotage the system. The orbital cortex receives the incoming stimuli. The hypothalamus, which is part of the information processing center, interprets the stimuli as dangerous and sends an alarm to the caudate nucleus, which is connected to the limbs of the body. The limbs are alerted to prepare for flight or fight. If the circuits are overloaded, the person may not be able to move at all. They will freeze instead of run. (See *The Case for Healing Manual* www. liferecovery.com.)

In obsessive-compulsive disorder (OCD), the orbital cortex sends a warning as a series of repeated false alarms. It is the job of the caudate nucleus to switch off the warning light. If the signal is not switched off in a

173

timely fashion, the alarm continues to cycle through the system, demanding action. This triggers the higher-thought processes to figure out what is wrong and come up with a solution. Any demonic interference with the caudate nucleus can keep the alarm flashing and produce an obsession in the mind as a demand for action.

Demonic interference in the caudate nucleus allows a stream of racing thoughts in the higher-level reasoning to pressure the mind to come up with a solution to silence the flashing alarm. If those thoughts were also controlled by a demon of *Confusion,* for example, it could suggest compulsive behaviors that afford no solution to the imagined danger. Out of desperation, those thoughts or behaviors are "waved through" by *Reasoning* and endorsed by our higher level of intellectual functioning, which then gives the Enemy permission to continue to apply the incessant pressure to fix the problem while simultaneously obstructing the solution to that problem.

When the relief sought by the body and mind of the person is not found, the failure of the system to solve the problem reinforces the obsessive/compulsive activities in the person's mind to try harder or repeat the failed-process again. This begins to form a new brain pathway and a pathological response to a simple occurrence. Not being able to control an external situation like being sneezed on, for example is now interpreted by *Fear* as being "germy" or feeling "dirty." These unresolved issues cause a loss of peace and tranquility to the internal mental functioning which causes *Anxiety* to begin to manifest at both a subconscious level and in the person's behavior.

Rather than resisting the agreement with the lie that *Fear* is tempting the person to believe, it is embraced.

This gives the Enemy permission to proceed. He creates a bogus solution to the problem that he has convinced us is a real problem that has now risen to the level of life threatening in our minds. His newly created compulsion then acts in response to the flashing-alarm system to mediate the situation. The flashing alarm has been conditioned to trigger that newly conditioned compulsion as a response to the obsession. This new behavior becomes etched into the brain to form a new brain pathway or track we call OCD.

Repeating the compulsive response to the alarm creates a pattern that infringes upon the person's ability to act spontaneously or move freely in their life. They are not able to adjust smoothly to the various demands place upon them by their external circumstances. They are obsessed with controlling those events. As a result they do not return to a state of peace and homeostasis because they are now controlled, caught up in the incessant demands that come flooding into their mind to get free from both the obsession and the compulsion to control the obsession. Eventually they become occupied only with getting high or finding the next fix to shut down the *Panic* and *Frustration*.

If the orbital cortex continues to fire frantic messages to the caudate nucleus and the "gear shifter" is stuck, the message of *Fear* and *Panic* will continue to be re-sent through the system, which programs the compulsion into their ordinary behavior. *Cravings* highlights the urgency creating a demand for the substance or to complete the act that will calm the circuits. The person's will has just been overpowered, tricked into cooperating with the solution of his demonic handler. The person has been seduced into believing that what they are doing is the corrective action necessary to relieve their pain or quiet their fear when, in fact it is an agreement with bondage.

If that corrective behavior does not succeed in turning the "warning light" off, the message continues to circulate madly through the system. This increases the pressure to find a solution. Thoughts and feelings are being formulated into actions that condition and control us into believing and acting on the lies *Fear* is telling us. The ultimate end of this is an out-of-control mental fatigue or a panic attack.

The Panic Button

As we have seen, not only can the Enemy sabotage the circuits, he can also interfere with the messages sent on those circuits. Sending information through a filter of fear and then "holding the gate open" so those fear messages recycle over and over creates a painful distraction that distresses the brain and causes *Panic*.

Panic is a sense of immanent death that sends an energy surge that overcharges the circuits and floods the individual with useless information. It raises the level of urgency. We are desperate to find the switch to turn off the "Panic Button." The emotional exhaustion and desire to stop the pain or fill the void creates a perfect storm in the mind of the victim. *Panic* intensifies *Addiction's* hold on us, which in turn, moves the obsessive thoughts to compulsive acts and more panicky feelings. *Pain* is the underlying motivator in many of these behaviors.

Pain is an electrical signal interpreted by our brain. Neuropathic pain is a chronic pain state that usually (but not always) is caused by some sort of tissue trauma. In neuropathic pain, the nerve fibers themselves are often damaged, dysfunctional or injured. These damaged nerve fibers send incorrect electrical signals to the brain's pain center. (Murphy, 2009)

-Dan Murphy, DC—Faculty Life Chiropractic College West; Vice President ICA 2003-2009; ICA Chiropractor of the Year 2009

Pain itself, though not often thought of as demonic can be. God has given us pain as a warning system to alert us to pay attention to certain conditions operating out of control in the body. Inflammation, infections, and broken bones are all legitimate functions of pain. Chronic, ongoing, excruciating torment and emotional pain, however, are not useful to our long-term wellbeing and therefore must be suspect as the work of the Enemy. Though they do draw attention to places where our hearts have been broken, only Jesus has power to heal the brokenhearted and set us free from the demonic torment of ongoing *Pain*.

Pain often creates the initial state of emergency which gives *Cravings* and *Addiction* permission to take over the management of our lives and usurp our privileges of free will under the guise of making us feel better. Feeling out of control is another familiar root in those who use chemicals as a means of managing their emotions. If these feelings of urgency are permitted to thrive, they begin to call the shots and create a psychological or physiological dependence on the substance that the user believes will help them cope with the pain or the obsession.

Those obsessions can be about any idea or a feeling that suits the Enemy's fancy. If we use the demonic solutions to find relief or deal with the pain or fix our emotions, we are caught in the matrix of the demonic programming that controls us against our wills. How will our feeble attempts to try and overcome prevail against our Enemy without the strength of the truth and the power of God defending us in these spiritual conflicts? (See *The Truth about Fear, Anxiety, and Panic Attacks* (CD) www. liferecovery.com.)

Addictions Are Strong Compulsions

Addictions are strong compulsions to use. *Cravings* are strong demands made upon the system to do or indulge in certain things *Fear* has convinced the mind to believe are essential to survival or relief. Once the Enemy's solution is accepted, our using or our eating or our rituals as prescribed by *Fear* become a mindless process.

Notice how physical needs and the requests for more energy or the desire to relieve pain are being solved with a set of equations that have been rewritten by *Trauma* and *Fear*. The mind has been coerced and conditioned into accepting these new solutions and uses them to run the mental and biological functions of the body more effectively. The new equation may read:

More sugar   = more energy
Caffeine   = energy to jumpstart the day

Over-the-counter meds	=	relaxing
Pills	=	pain relief
Junk food	=	comfort
Cookies	=	love, home, and family
Drugs	=	symptom management
Alcohol	=	fun, feel better, a way to fit in, decrease apprehension, and control emotions

From this, it would appear that *Cravings* can be introduced into the biological systems at either a physiological or psychological level. Because we are fearfully and wonderfully made, freedom and health operate at levels far beyond mere willpower. The neuro-pathways, the orbital cortex, the cingulated gyrus, the caudate nucleus, and as yet many other unidentified parts and functions of the brain and body that control movement and behavior make our bodies more vulnerable to spiritual interference than we realize. This understanding adds weight to the argument that recovery is less about human determination, will-power, and self-control and more a matter of deliverance.

- What are some of the equations that run your systems?
- Is it possible that the battle to quit using is more spiritual than you first believed?
- What is your responsibility in this thing if you are controlled by something you cannot stop yourself from doing?
- Does this mean you are just helplessly bound and meant to be addicted all your life?

- Could it be that the Enemy has been messing with your brain to set up OCD or other compulsive behaviors in you that you hate doing but cannot stop?
- Could you be suffering from a mineral deficiency that creates a craving for sugar or alcohol (that turns to sugar) in the bloodstream? What would keep you from taking a liquid mineral supplement to correct that deficiency?

Chapter 16

Scientific Proof God Was Right!

We are fearfully and wonderfully made; a three-part being made up of body, soul, and spirit. To the smallest detail of our being, our body was designed by the Creator to live and function in such a way as to not only sustain and regenerate itself but to also provide a place of suitable habitation for our soul and spirit. Because these parts must remain connected, the health of the body is critical for the optimum functioning of the spiritual man.

To maintain the health of the body, God provided a strict set of instructions in the owner's manual, including the nourishment necessary to fuel and rebuild it. The importance of having the right fuel is reflected in God making it a priority in the list of instructions to Adam in the Garden. Because the food we eat is essential in sustaining the continuity and function of the body's frequencies, food becomes a critical piece in spiritual warfare.

Doing our part to ensure the health and victory of the whole comes down to eating good food.

In the first commandment God told the couple to be fruitful and multiply. In the second commandment He told them what to eat, instructing them on what was necessary for maintaining the life of both the body and soul it carried. Science is just now confirming what God knew all along: that the energy levels in the body are directly related to the frequency levels of the foods eaten. The Maker of man identified those foods as the green herb and the fruit with the seed in it. Science agrees that they provide us with our greatest sources of high frequency, high-octane fuel. (See Gen. 1:29–30.)

As we have already seen in the study of frequencies, the frequencies of substances we eat, breathe, and absorb are critical to health. Many pollutants have low frequencies, and cause the body's healthy frequencies to be lowered and weakened. ...Fresh produce has up to 15 Hz; dry herbs from 12 to 22 Hz; and fresh herbs from 20 to 27 Hz. Essential oil frequencies start at 52 Hz and go as high as 320 Hz, which is the frequency of Rose Oil. These higher frequencies create an environment in which disease, bacteria, virus, fungus, and cancers often cannot live.

When we eat food our body breaks down the food particles into colloids. These nutrient particles contain the energy, (in the form of an electrical charge), measured as frequencies that are transported to our cells via the circulatory system.

Your body's cells communicate with each other with pulses of Electricity. When we eat food our body breaks down the food particles into there Smallest size (COLLOIDS). A colloid is the smallest possible form of nutrient particle (generally–The size ranges from .01 to .00001 of a micron in diameter).

Article Source: http://EzineArticles.com/1421536
Electromagnetic Charges in Food! by James Spicer
Submitted On August 20, 2008

Article Source: http://EzineArticles. com/?expert=-
James_Spicer Article Source: http://EzineArticles.
com/1421536

Eating foods with higher frequencies supplies more of what the body needs to be energized and remain active. Processed foods, including fast food, have lower frequencies and thus produce less energy. Eating foods not on God's recommended "Food List" deprives the body of the electrical energy it needs to run all its functions at an optimum level. It would be like trying to run your machinery at half power or your electrical appliances and lights at lower amperage and expecting the same output of power and light.

The Sounds of Music

Others have confirmed and implemented another fascinating discovery about frequencies and how the individual organs of the body each make their own sound or individual musical note.

VoiceBio©™ functions on the principal that the human voice, apart from being a communication medium, also exhibits all of the silent and audible working frequencies of the body, mind and emotions. While there are 12 essential sound frequencies which make up and define human energetics, a majority of individuals have missing or stressed "notes" which correlate with weakened brain patterns. Weakened brain patterns translate to compromised health and impaired regenerative abilities.

VoiceBio—Frequency & the Body
http://www.voicebio. com/freq-and-body.php

Frequencies are vibrations. Vibrations create sounds. Sound is made up of frequencies that are vibrations. Because everything in the Universe has its own specific vibration or frequencies, everything in the universe also has its own sound, including our physical body. If everything that has a frequency, including our body, emits its own sound, then the individual organs of the body should also be able to be identified by the specific "sound" each other is making. Which leads us to the question; could this be the way the cells and organs in our body communicate with each other in order to keep the life-processes of the body flowing smoothly?

It may very well be that the distinction of frequencies is what gives the body this amazing and necessary ability to communicate with itself. Frequencies are measured in Megahertz, the measure of electro-chemical vibrations per second. A continuous stream of electromagnetic current sends signals throughout the nervous system, which allows the members of the body, the brain, heart, and so on to communicate with each other. Frequencies and the change in frequencies create the language that allows the members of the body to "talk" to one another. This is what the proponents of Voicebio believe.

The various parts of the body attract resources and communicate with each other by way of sound frequency. In other words, each organ has its own keynote frequency that resonates to the particular nutrients, minerals and sound vibration required for function. As an example, the colon vibrates to the note of B, while the liver vibrates to the note of G. Fortunately, for our sanity, the frequencies of our organs and systems function outside the range of human hearing. There are in all, 12 keynote frequencies present in the human body:

C C# D D# E F F# G G# A A# B

The keynote frequencies found in the body are the very same frequencies found in music. And just as the note of C appears several times on a piano keyboard at varying octaves, the note of C appears many times in the body. The voice, being the composite sound of the human being, is representative of all of the frequencies in the body.

VoiceBio—Frequency & the Body
http://www.voicebio.com/freq-and-body.php

Scientific evidence also seems to support the idea that each organ and thought and emotion has its own distinct frequency, and that those specific vibrations correspond to the keys on the musical scale. The sounds of the twelve notes on the musical scale and their octaves match the sounds made by the organs of the body with each organ's health being determined by how "in tune" it is with its keynote.

Could it be that, as our body is thinking and feeling and functioning, it is singing to itself? The blending of those various sounds comes into unison to create the one sound that becomes the sound of our own voice. It could be said that the sound of our voice is like a melody and our life becomes a symphony of its parts. As the various members or our body make music together, we live. When they cease to sing, we die. Truly, we are fearfully and wonderfully made!

Our bodies are literally filled with instruments, each playing part of the melody that makes our life a constant song in the ears of our Father. Each moment we live, He is conscious of us as He hears the sound of our voice being lifted up, even when we are not speaking. As we offer Him the sacrifice of praise, He hears the cry of our heart coming from the very sounds of our body as it lives. We are not alone.

All of creation seems to have been given a voice. This would make perfect sense since everything has frequencies and frequencies are vibrations that make sounds. Could this be why the Bible says the "rocks will cry out" (Lu. 19:40) and the "wilderness lifts up its voice"? Which leads us to believe that if the stars sing and the trees and rivers clap their hands, our lives may be more poetic than we think. What at first may have appeared to be allegorical may just as rightly be understood as both biblical and literal.

Putting Wrong Things in; Keeping Right Things Out

Because the destruction of the body becomes one of Satan's primary targets and because the body must have certain types of fuel (food) to maintain healthy frequencies and because those frequencies are determined by the foods we eat, manipulation and contamination of our food sources, the soil, and its production, have become one of his most coveted methods of covert activity.

The severity of the problem increases when we add medications and mood-altering substances to the mix. Factoring in our free will increases the margin of error to the possibility of one hundred percent. We get to make a choice regarding whether the body will get those things it must have to live victoriously or be betrayed. If the Devil can condition us to believe eating healthy food is not spiritually relevant but, rather, a matter of personal choice or preferred taste, he can control our decisions even while we are being deceived into believing we are exercising our free will to eat what we want. Removing all cause for spiritual alarm regarding the foods we eat or the substances we ingest has given us the dubious honor of being put us in charge of our own destruction.

The Enemy has already conditioned us to believe we can comfort ourselves by putting things into our mouths. Now all he has to do is alter our belief about what is good and desirable. If he can impair or manipulate our taste buds to crave sweet things or create an aversion for vegetables or dislike certain textures of healthy God-made foods, he has accomplished all he needed to in one mere moment. We are oblivious, indulgent, and fooled into feeling invincible and empowered to eat the things we want. *Rebellion* ties the final knot with a simple little suggestion: "Oh, Yuck! I don't like the taste of_____" or "Don't tell me what I can or cannot or eat!"

Because the things we put into our bodies carry frequencies, they have the power to hurt or heal by altering the strength of our body's energy flow. The Enemy knows about frequencies. Eating processed foods, junk foods, drinking soda and alcohol, injecting drugs, and taking too many over-the-counter medications can deprive our body of the nutrients it needs to sustain health and plug it up with toxins.

Depriving ourselves of necessary vitamins and minerals hinders the production of neurotransmitters, amino acids, and other vital elements for health while restricting the energy the body needs to function well. This takedown of the body only exacerbates the problem and makes us an easier spiritual target in the end.

Nonetheless, because most of us are not convinced that what we eat is all that relevant, we continue to eat what we want. We may feel good for a moment because it tastes good or because it boosts our energy, but the "high" is short-lived and ultimately empty. Just as quickly as we feel good, we begin to feel tired, lethargic, foggy, and crabby.

The loss of energy brings with it a new set of lower lows and the depletion of dopamine and serotonin, which sets up a craving for more of the "something" that elevates our mood and makes us feel better. The cycle goes around again. Eventually, we lose our excitement for life outside of the drug or the food we want. We become consumed with getting it, only to become consumed with the program or the diet we have put ourselves on to get rid of it.

Treatment and dieting are multibillion-dollar businesses in this country. To lose X number of pounds or get sober becomes a more pressing personal goal as meaning and purpose shrink from our lives. Happiness and meaning have become redefined as a magical weight at which I will be okay, loved, beautiful, and perfect! Though a healthy weight does improve health and often our body image, do not be disillusioned into thinking that losing the weight or being perfectly in control of your calorie intake is the key to your search for meaning.

- What is your magical "happiness" weight? Twenty to two hundred pounds less than you weigh right now?
- Define meaning in your life.
- How willing are you to let go of eating habits that are decreasing your vitality?

Chapter 17

Beware! Strings Attached

Beating the addictions and weight management are two of *Craving's* most commonly assigned tasks. It is one of his favorite tactics for defining and destroying people. Because most people never suspect their problems to be related to a spiritual force or source behind the craving, they are quick to accept full responsibility for their behavior. They become consumed trying to curb, stop, overcome, or change their actions, often at great expense to themselves and others.

Though most would not deny the power of a poor diet and lack of good nutrition as part of the problem, they fail to see the interconnected correlation between one's spiritual and physical health. If we fail to see the relationship between biological balances and the depletion of essential minerals, for example, all of our systems will be in jeopardy. Failing to make the nutrition connection between our physical health and sense of wellbeing and the spiritual forces of demonic activity behind the problems, cause many to chase the wrong solutions in trying to regain health and vitality.

Many of us think we should just be happy and feel good in spite of what we feed our body or how we treat it. The domino effect of lies, poor diets, drug use, hormonal imbalances, low energy, and high stress lifestyles begin to compromise the body's functioning at every level, including our emotional and spiritual health. Most of us would not attribute our health crisis to something as unfamiliar as a demonic spirit or something as seemingly innocent and familiar as eating a bowl of sugary breakfast cereal like the ones we grew up on.

Plugging in Substitutes

Our minds have come to accept thousands of alterations, adaptations, and substitutes that have been plugged into the original equation and operating systems written by God. They are embraced as more appealing or easier and faster because they offer us a shortcut or quick fix for getting our needs met. But alas, everything has a price.

Altering the natural process always has spiritual consequences, though we often fail to connect them, (at least at first), with the underlying energy drain we experience when we use them. That first moment of anxiety relief, that first drag on the cigarette, that first burst of sweetness or that initial high or "aha" seem to stick in our minds, binding us to using them yet again while blinding us to the after-effects or the long-term results of those substances.

We prefer to not be bothered and do not want to know the facts, believing ignorance is absolution from involvement. As long as we can keep the discussion of our problems in the realm of the natural, that is, what I want, like, or choose to do, we think we can control them. As long as we think we can control them through diets and programs and pills, we think we are in control and being responsible in doing something positive to help ourselves.

As long as we can hold fear and pain at bay and avoid going into the place of the spiritually unknown, we think we are safe. But if our need for safety is defined as a need to stay ignorant or as a need to control, it will create greater anxiety that will lock us into a humanistic paradigm, where *we* are our only solution. Being our own solution, as we will discover, is nothing more than a setup for fatigue and failure that creates an open door for the familiar spirits to come in and bind us at a deeper level of spiritual deception as they attempt to assist us in our dilemma.

If taking control is the only approach we can take to our out-of-control behavior of eating, spending, hoarding, using, and trying, then we will live going into an ever-deepening pit of *Pain* and *Fear,* controlled by the very behaviors we are trying to control.

Why Are We So Clueless?

Rarely do we suspect the craving to be the work of a spirit or driven by a demonic agenda. If most of us would agree, at least in theory, that we want to eat right and we know what is healthy and we have no lack of information on good nutrition or people who will help us eat right, then why do we have so much trouble eating good food and avoiding the junk?

Where is the resistance to healthy eating and obedient living coming from? Would it be to our advantage to explore the reality of the thing that silently opposes us in our efforts to stay clean and get sober and lose some weight? Where does that unidentified resistance we slough off as no big deal, my sweet tooth, or whatever, really come from? Comments like these raise the question: Is there anything that operates on a purely natural plane without being influenced, at least to some degree, by the spiritual forces which surround it?

Human nature seems to drift along in a semi-comfortable state of inertia. As long as things go well and life is good, we are emboldened to reject as minor and arbitrary, the relevance of spiritual influences on our own personal world. That's not the way things operate, you say. Believing what we want to believe may work on the surface of human life and existence until we get down to the level of pain and sickness where life is out of control. There we discover, as did one reformed atheist: "I did not control squat."

So What Is the Real Problem?

The problem is that we think it is up to us to take responsibility to fix this mess or get control of this thing we are doing. We are strongly motivated because we hate the things we see ourselves doing. We have completely bought into the lie that Satan regularly uses to define us using the axiom that "we are what we do." Not realizing the error of this belief we fail to receive the truth, that God defined us according to His Word and made us in His image. We beat ourselves up because we are not able to do or stop doing what it is we see ourselves doing that we hate.

Both doing and not doing present us with a similar problem, in that both tend to put all the pressure back on us. In the midst of the battle we are in jeopardy of refusing God's help by exchanging our rest and reliance upon God for the help from another self-help formula for success. The Enemy uses all of this to set up the possibilities for more failure, making to sober up or lose the weight a preoccupation that only opens the door to more failure, frustration, and feelings of *Guilt* and *Self-Condemnation*.

The "stinkin' thinkin'" of *Self-Condemnation* and *Comparison* trap us in the futility of thinking nothing is ever going to change. Linking up with other negative ideas and attitudes creates an acidic environment in our bodies and death to our souls. Without the divine intervention of deliverance that the Apostle Paul cried out for in the midst of his miserable condition, the hope of lasting change without a contrite heart is remote.

The Bible's antidote to negativism and the defeat of recycling the feelings of futility is praise and thanksgiving. The Bible invites us to "think upon whatsoever things are lovely and just and of good report" (Phil. 4:8). Deliverance begins with crying out to God, "Who will deliver me from this Body of Death?"

Meditating on regrets, the trouble in our life, the opinions of others, or our past failures only triggers the synthesizing of an enzyme in the body that cements *Fear* and *Negativity* into our long-term memory bank. This allows it to become part of a permanent filter that alters our way of looking at and dealing with every other thing that pops up in our lives.

Negative thoughts and emotions bind together to form a fear filter that then becomes part of the grid through which we process incoming information. If all the information coming into the brain is viewed through dark-colored glasses, it will all be tainted gray. The result will be a message of fear and stress that becomes part of every new idea and image and creates a new processing system through which we filter future information.

Thus, our future dims and our hope sets before the Son can "rise with healing in His wings" (Mal. 4:2). *Fear* and *Anxiety* begin to affect and manipulate the physical systems of the body, including the glandular and nervous systems, which disseminate information and execute enforcement of their safety commands. Not being aware of the spiritual takeover of our physical communication systems allows those spirits to expand their territories and root deeper into our other organs and biological functions.

We are becoming less aware of these spiritual influences as we become more dependent on them. They begin to feel familiar. Their manipulation of our systems to solve the irresolvable conflicts they have set up to bind us feel like nothing different than we ourselves making the choice to use or eat or try to stop eating and using. We have unconsciously come into agreement with the lie. I have become convinced that the thing I am doing is me and that the activities are my own thoughts and actions.

Good Old Willpower and Gumption

Once the Enemy is in control of sending and receiving the messages, the issue of change and recovery or sobriety or any kind of personal improvement moves from one of personal resolve and willpower to one of deliverance. No amount of self-discipline or personal effort will work to release us from the grip of the spirit of *Craving, Addiction,* or *Lust*. It does not matter how much our human trainers would tell us, "You can do it!" What was once your choice has now become the Enemy's option, and you have become his slave.

If *Addiction* wants to smoke, we will smoke for him, deceived into not only buying expensive cigarettes for him with our own money, but persuaded to believe it is our idea because we agree with the thought, "I like to smoke." If the Enemy can convince us that smoking is all our idea, what more does he have to convince us of? That thinking will operate in our mind and body until we wake up and make a decision contrary to the *spirit of Nicotine,* and declare, "I want to quit." Even making that new declaration of wanting to quit, our priority does not resolve the battle raging within, though our new intention is firm.

But, if it was "all me" and my idea to smoke in the first place, we would think changing our mind should not be that big of a deal. So, why is it? The difficulty of making the change should tell us something about how much freedom and control we really had in the first place. It would appear that the freedom we were exercising was an illusion. A veil had been used to cover the clandestine operations of the Enemy whose whole intention the entire time was to take us down using our own volition and willpower to do it. And then when we fail to quit, he can strike us down with accusations of guilt and poor self-discipline. How clever is that!

The fact that we are not in control, though we thought we were, is called deception. We were programmed, brainwashed, and indoctrinated. The continued participation in the act is called slavery. This is why straight treatment and dieting do not work. We are bound, first in doing the thing we think we want to do, then in trying to stop doing something we do not want to do, hooked, addicted, and obviously, miserable. If changing or quitting were a simple matter of willpower, just wanting to be free should have been enough to set us free immediately. We must admit that what is binding and holding us back is bigger than we are or our willpower to overcome it. We are still being controlled by something beyond us. (See *Breaking the Cycle* (two-CD set) www.liferecovery.com.)

Chapter 18

Willpower and Treatment

M ost treatment programs, including many that claim
to be Christian, are based on what I call "the med-
ical/will-power model." On the one hand they tell you
that if you are addicted, it is not your fault and you will
not be judged because you have a disease.

On the other hand, once you enter the program, you
are told that if you want sobriety you can have it if you
just work hard enough. If you fail, you are judged for
not wanting it badly enough or that you are not working
hard enough or that you are just not being serious enough
about recovery. In other words, if you fail the program,
it is not the program's fault. It is your fault, and you will
be judged accordingly.

Two assumptions are made using the medical/will-
power model. The first is that using toxic, mood-altering
substances is a disease. Second, it is up to you to quit. A
great deal of confusion and judgment are attached to the
medical/disease model of treatment. That model says that

the addiction is a sickness; therefore, you are not responsible for being sick, and it is not your fault. You cannot help yourself. It is not up to you to get well.

If that is true, then the way we handle the disease of alcoholism or addictions makes no sense. If the problem is a disease over which you have no control, and "it is not your fault," and the purpose of the problem being labeled a disease is to relieve the victim from any uncomfortable feelings of guilt or of being judged, then why do we turn around and make the person feel guilty and responsible for the outcome of our willpower, shame-based treatment programs?

In the medical model, if you cannot get rid of cancer by an act of your will, you are not judged as bad or treated unkindly. As a matter of fact, all the more care and kindness are shown to you. In the treatment models for addiction, if it is truly a disease, why are you judged for not being serious about your sobriety or working the program hard enough or go to enough meetings? What began as not your fault ends up being all your fault.

But how can I kick the habit if the habit is a disease? Is my problem that I have a habit-forming disease? What ever happened to the nonjudgmental intentions of the disease model that has, all of a sudden, slipped into a matter of moral judgment without ever saying it? I am told I need more willpower and must try harder, which ultimately makes it my fault that I have a disease.

As you can see, the logic of the program is not consistent within itself. If the rationale does not carry through from the beginning to the end in a client's mind, how will the steps of the program make much sense or lead them to any credible or successful conclusion? The logic flips from: "It's a disease, and it's not your fault," to "You did not try hard enough, and it is your fault." So which is it?

Integrating the concept of God into a treatment program can be another point of confusion in the diabolical strategy of the Enemy to make us doubt the love and power of God. Unless the spiritual concepts included in the program are "rightly divided" (1 Tim. 2:15; 3:16) and presented in the context of the biblical doctrine of spiritual warfare, confusion and condemnation can be the result. Most of the treatment programs are shame-based even if they initially deny it. If the treatment program happens to be Christian-based, the shame and guilt of failure is exponentially increased with the thought that, "Not even God can help me" or, "Now even God is mad at me." The conclusion is that I must really be bad and beyond help.

Regardless of the substance in question, the answer is the same. No sophisticated treatment programs, dieting plans, or nutritional supplementation, even administered with the greatest of good will and intention, will be enough to rout the body of death system that is operating under the surface. Ignoring the spiritual forces behind the *Addiction* and using the program approach with their abstinence, dieting, and self-improvement plans has become our major approach to out-of-control anything.

Designed to deal with only the behavior of the diseased, they do nothing to address the spiritual forces that lie hidden within that are enslaving the addicted. The solution must include a revelation of the root lie and the truth about using in the first place. It must include truth and deliverance from the demonic impersonators who have guised themselves as us. This comes through the work of the Holy Spirit in us, searching our souls to show us what *Destruction* has done under the pretenses of helping us, and what *Darkness* has done under the guise of enlightening us.

A New Normal

We are so used to taking the responsibility and trying harder that we do not even question the outcome of such assumptions. We fail until failing becomes the "new normal." We give up and decide to do the best we can and live with things the way they are. Feeling disappointed in ourselves and in God creates a whole new level of hopelessness.

We are locked into the place where we go in circles. The vicious cycle goes around again. We accept what we cannot change and learn to live with the lie, not able to see anything different than the mindset we've been living in, which is the very mindset the Enemy uses to keep the old patterns going.

I Did It Myself

Everyone that has successfully broken free from the control of these demonic beings has done so only by embracing the revelation of Jesus Christ specific to their situation. That revelation set them free to choose truth and cry out for deliverance. Many give the glory and praise for their release to God. Some attribute their freedom to some form of God they acknowledge as a power higher than themselves. This is another tremendous problem and place of error, another slippery slope where the Enemy is trying to usurp the glory of God for himself. Through another act of our will, we have fallen for the deception and chosen poorly. We have handed God's glory to another and given our freedoms over to an imposter.

The bottom line on using and not using is to know that we were not created to use these foreign substances in the first place. When it is a matter of food, we were not created to live on junk food. We were not created to be an alcoholic or a glutton. Our true identity is not in describing ourselves as addicts or users or losers or as overweight or food junkies. We are created in the image of God as one of His sons or daughters.

We are not born knowing that we know that, and because we are born only knowing what we are taught, what we learn from the "snake pit" obscures the truth about who we really are. Our divine nature is our first nature. The Enemy has psychologically reconditioned us to believe we are what we do, think, feel, say, and what other people say about us. We are reintroduced to the truth about who we really are when the Holy Spirit introduces us to Jesus Christ. Only then can the truth be known. Only then can we begin to become who God had always intended us to be.

That revelation reconnects me with who I am in Christ and who He has known me to be since before the foundation of the world. Before I ever "am," He knew who I was. Knowing that I am known connects me with who I am in Christ, so that I can be restored to true sonship and fellowship with my Father in heaven. It connects me with who He intended me to be from the beginning and causes me to walk in the power and love and Spirit of

Him who lives to free me from the bondage of Satan. He is the One True God who cannot be worshiped except in spirit and truth.

Managing Cravings Is Not Freedom from Them

Many do not see the attempt to manage *Cravings* as an exercise in futility. They dive into the latest self-help and self-improvement books and courses and diet magazines and Do-It-Yourself Life for Dummies manuals, all of which feed right into the independent "it's up to me" mentality. From a natural point of view, these seem like commendable solutions. Though there is an element of cooperation required in the rescue of even the most helpless among us, trying to curb *Cravings* on our own can become a vicious circle.

When we denounce that God played any part in our recovery and attribute our freedom to our own willpower, we are still carrying the burden of our sobriety or weight loss on our own shoulders. Real victory does not come in white-knuckling it or counting days of sobriety or counting calories. True victory must include a realization of knowing that we are really free. Using was never who I was in the first place. True victory is knowing that "if the Son makes you free, you shall be free indeed" (Jn. 8:36). Crediting our sobriety to our own willpower or the loss of poundage to our diet only makes us continually responsible to stay sober or slim ourselves.

That is not real freedom. It is hypervigilance that requires continued effort and energy to maintain our current status through self-management and support groups or systems. Why go through all the effort of self-management, which is an illusion anyway, when obedience and deliverance would serve us much better? (See *Answers to Prayer* (two-CD set) <u>www.liferecovery.com</u>.)

Chapter 19

The Vicious Cycle

The vicious cycle that controls us often begins with a sense of vague disquieting, a decreased sense of well-being or apprehension we will call unidentified anxiety. Because it often lurks under the surface of conscious thought and activity, it remains unidentified and its source undetermined. We begin to grasp for things to fill the emptiness. We look for ways to distract ourselves from the boredom and calm ourselves or provide an outlet for our pent up stress, anger, stuffed emotions and unused energy.

We feel ourselves becoming more despondent or more aggressive in dealing with the problem. Through a redefined set of conditioned responses based on experiences and the reinforcements made by *Fear,* we have learned we need to and can manage the pain, boredom, and anxiety on our own if we eat, shop, gamble, drink, smoke, cut ourselves, or indulge in any number of other real or imagined escapes.

Any success, defined as some sense of temporary relief, conditions us to be willing to try that same thing again the next time the need presents itself. Many, if not all of these temporary fixes, entice us to make agreements with things that are detrimental and binding, offering a small relief for a slight exchange of more and more of our life and our freedom. We are at risk to be overtaken by *Cravings* and *Control*.

After we have given in and done the thing we promised ourselves we would not do again (relapse), we take the other side of the torture rack and begin to blame ourselves or someone else for our using. *Self-condemnation* and all the other "I should have/shouldn't have" debaters from Hell line up to beat us up in our minds.

This misery creates the next round of unidentified *Anxiety,* only this time the added weight of *Guilt* presses down on us to make the burden even greater and the need for relief even more urgent. We give into the *Cravings* and use, not yet ready to admit that we are being controlled by those *Cravings*.

Certain that we do not have a problem; we fail to call out for help or admit we cannot help ourselves. We absent-mindedly tell ourselves we can stop any time we want, only to find ourselves using more than ever. We go around again in the vicious cycle determined to diet, exercise, and count calories until we become consumed with quitting or counting or trying not to think about what we think that we should not be thinking about until we collapse!

Admitting I have a problem is the first step to solving the problem. It is not so much a matter of taking responsibility as it is looking honestly at what is going on without denying or downplaying the situation and asking God to deliver me. For some of us, our deliverance will be just that simple. We will ask, and it will be done.

Others will ask and probably have asked many times before, though their pleas seem to fall on deaf ears. Those who receive are not more favored than those who wait. They are not more loved or better or more deserving or have more faith than those who struggle. The difference has more to do with what we believe to be true about God and how we see ourselves than anything else.

The besetting thought "What is wrong with me?" sets in motion a series of lies and gives us the first clue to the Enemy's agenda to get us to doubt the love of God for us. The lie that "God doesn't care about me" ties into the idea that "nothing ever changes." But if we are going to "take every thought captive" (2 Cor. 10:4–5) then we must ask ourselves where do *Doubt* and *Condemnation* and *Self-pity* come from, Heaven or Hell? If the answer is Hell, then the question becomes, what is their real plot against us and why are we still listening to them?

Dieting

Dieting is a trap. Because we do not get the results we were praying for, we decide to take matters into our own hands. One of the most popular forms of self-directed deliverance is called dieting. Considering addictions and getting victory over them from a spiritual point of view sheds new light on the subject of being set free from any life-controlling habit in which we might find ourselves ensnared, including dieting.

Before we begin the discussion of dieting, let us define the word. Dieting is that which is typically understood to mean the regulation of one's intake of food for the express purpose of manipulating the outcomes of weight gain and loss. We are not using the word *diet* to mean the necessary intake of food or the modification of a diet for the purposes of supplementing our food intake to rebuild our health.

Denial, self-discipline, and dieting are household words to most of us and often recommended as steps to weight loss or to regain control of eating habits that have gotten out of control. Though billions of dollars are invested each year in the latest dieting fad or medical breakthrough to lose weight, most are only schemes and setups for more destruction. There are no quick fixes or shortcuts through the woods to get back to health. Health is the byproduct of obedient eating, not dieting.

The right path is really the same one it has always been. Submission and obedience to what God says about how and what to eat are the keys to life and vitality. Dieting is as legalistic as it is stressful. Notice that the first three letters of the word *dieting* spell the word "die." Jesus said that, *"It is the Spirit who gives life, the flesh profits nothing"* (Jn. 6:63). Dieting only depletes our body of what it is already deficient in by depriving it of what it desperately needs to function well. The more we diet, the more we mess up our metabolism. We take matters into our own hands, seeking advice from the latest diet masters or the newest health guru instead of the Lord.

Starvation

Starving ourselves to lose weight is extreme dieting and masks a stronghold of *Self-hatred*. *Control* and *Self-improvement* are part of the rationale for setting up an artificially created state of emergency in the body. When starvation or its milder version of dieting is used as a solution to eating disorders, it actually creates a state of emergency in the body. This causes the body to hold on to and hoard its food as fat in anticipation of the food famine it is experiencing.

The loss of energy through starvation and deprivation sends signals to the brain that interprets the situation as desperate. The body is instructed to store and stockpile the fat that we are trying to burn off through dieting, and we find ourselves stuck in that "gotta lose weight/can't lose weight" cycle. (Some believe that the fat is storing the poisonous toxins of the body to keep them from killing us.) Many have believed the lies of dieting and practiced the weight-loss schemes for so long that the natural rhythm of their metabolism may need divine healing in order to be restored to proper functioning.

Dieting is the unnatural attempt to manipulate and manage our body in a manner contrary to its original operating instructions. The results of trying to force ourselves to submit to any number of artificial dieting schemes, guided imagery, meditation, or spiritual exercises are as doomed to fail as we are determined to think they will work. Food eaten with guilt is as sure to bring upon us a demonic judgment, which may include weight gain, as the worshipping of food snares us into idolatry.

As with any other spiritual matter, rebellion against God's commands for eating can bring us into judgment for our rejection of the Gospel of Grace. *Rebellion* and embracing a religion of works has caused our tables to become a snare and a trap (Ro. 11:9–10). Dieting is one of those controlling obsessions that never bring us to a place of rest. Instead, it has replaced table grace and gratitude with *Gluttony* and *Guilt* or both.

Submission to the will of God and His prescription for health become our only sure and lasting hope for freedom. Managing *Cravings* is not freedom. Going to meetings for the rest of your life is not freedom. Freedom has nothing to do with willpower! Freedom is the absence of being preoccupied or obsessed by the substance, be it food or drugs. Freedom removes the programming that has locked us in failure, frustration, and fatigue. Freedom sets us free to serve with strength and peace and in obedience to the Word of God.

- How have temptation and desire been used to defeat you in your fight with craving and addiction?
- What are some of the latest gadget or gimmick or diets on "how to" that have caught your eye?
- Can you identify where you are on craving's vicious cycle?
- What excuses are worth using that risk the loss of our own soul?
- We are taught to pray expectantly—what do you expect when you pray? If you expect nothing that is most likely what you will get.
- Where does the rubber meet the road? Are we coming to a screeching halt, or is this thing never going to stop going round and round? It depends on who is in control of your appetites and actions.
- Are you opposed to considering deliverance as a means to your healing?

Chapter 20

Frog Soup

The quest that began with simply trying to numb the pain or lose the weight has come full circle. Denying our feelings, stuffing them down with food, or choosing to live with what we thought would be a better life without feelings, has turned into a nightmare. We are being consumed with the fear of trying to manage the pain we are now being forced to live with while *Isolation* and *Despair* and the absence of love are bringing us to a place of being too afraid to live.

We have medicated the pain of the soul with every manner of substance known to man until the fear of life is only surpassed by our attempts to escape it. Our pursuit of pain-killing substances as life's main focus now becomes life's main challenge. "Where can I get more of what I think it is I must have to satisfy this craving?" gives way to "I've got to stop using," or "go on a diet," or "get control of this thing before it kills me."

Not Just about More Willpower

Though I do not advocate decadence, the insidious grip of the Enemy pins us to the wall. We are up against more than just a situation that calls for more willpower since we have basically all tried that x number of times already. We are involved in a battle where we are no match for our opponent. We need rescue and deliverance, not another "you can do it" pep talk before we get back into the ring.

There is no shame in needing deliverance. Deliverance is part of the covenant Christ has made with us to not only save us but to set us free. All we have to do is believe the truth, ask for God's help, and receive it. But if we do not believe the Enemy is in the midst of our struggle, we will never ask for deliverance and if we never ask, we will go undelivered and die in our sin. Please make the correct biblical distinction here; dying in our sins is not synonymous with going to hell.

Absolution Is No Solution

Though the absolutes of countless rules and programs and diet plans and taking more responsibility are not the solution, neither is perverted grace. We are not looking for a way to absolve ourselves from responsibility or excuse indulgence or embrace perverted grace or a false peace.

How many times have we given into what we vowed we would never do again, only to do it again? We carefully count our calories all day only to splurge as a reward at the end of the day and then end up blaming ourselves and feeling guilty for eating. Eating becomes our preoccupation and food becomes our idol. The cycle must be broken.

We begin to hate ourselves for being too fat or too weak or too bad, or we readjust our definition of fat, weak, and bad to mean normal, so we are not as fat or weak or bad as we thought we were. The freedom to change the rules, the definitions of truth, and the standards of health give us an artificial outlook on our condition and only temporary relief. We are only learning to live with the lie.

As much as we change definitions and standards and dress sizes so we can accept ourselves as "okay," our manipulation of truth, nonetheless, does not stop millions of us from evolving into a population of sickly, lost, and confused souls. The commitment to stop using often swings in the other direction, giving us permission to live with passivity and accept a perverted form of grace that is not grace at all, but a license to sin.

We are losing our will to live without even knowing it. The struggle is exhausting, and because we have refused God's grace, it looks easier to succumb. *Death* begins with a low-key casual thought like "It's no big deal," or "It is what it is," and ends with "I hate my life; I wish I were dead." If that is true I might as well just go with the flow and get used to it. But the compromise does not stop with our acceptance of *Addiction* because the Enemy is never satisfied until we are destroyed and our bodies are in the grave.

Demonic Programming—A Summary

Our body is a God-made life support system that is vulnerable and accessible by both the powers of darkness and the truth of God. Satan uses our God-given learning and warning systems to teach us bad things. He is a master psychologist. He uses our legitimate needs for food, love, meaning, and relationships, to put pressure on us to choose badly.

He sets us up with pain or problems and then offers us false comforts and counterfeit solutions to address those needs. He uses things like food and fun, things connected with positive experiences, and wires them, a pleasant thing, together with a bad thing, to write new equations in our operating systems. This creates confusion and dissonance in both the biological systems and in our souls. We are forced to compromise our goodness and give up our innocence to get love. We agree to silence the truth in order to be accepted.

The Enemy then uses negative experiences to reinforce the habit of sinning, the main behavior he has been trying to set up in our lives since the beginning. Knowing we hate sin and pain and rejection, he uses a negative experience to persuade us to believe a lie and blackmails us into continuing to do what we hate to avoid withdrawal, retaliation, or ridicule. He uses our memories to hold the pain in place and keep us in line.

This programming begins at the moment of conception and continues as long as it is permitted. Many of us never suspect such a deep and diabolical plot against us and act more like trained dogs than sons and daughters of God, even after we are saved. We have been conditioned to avoid the momentary discomforts of following righteousness in order to engage in activities promising immediate gratification. If all life is about is how to avoid suffering and how to indulge the appetites, Satan will have a splendid time of it, sailing his cruise ship on the tide of our carnal appetites.

The Keys to Freedom

The first key to freedom is deliverance. Deliverance acknowledges that we cannot do it ourselves, but like Paul, we acknowledge our very wretchedness and misery as evidence that we do not agree with the forces the Enemy is using to tempt us to sin. The very fact that we feel guilty for sinning proves we were not built to sin in the first place. The Devil cheats! Coercion and control do not permit us the true exercise of our free will to choose not to sin.

The second key is to realize, through a revelation from the Spirit of Truth, that we are not built by God to *use* in the first place. Using is *not* who we are, though our members are performing the act. Paul says in Romans 7:18 "For I know that in me (that is, in my flesh) nothing good dwells; for to will is present with me, but how to perform what is good I do not find." When we understand that, we realize we are *already* free. We were built free and brought back to freedom through the death and resurrection of Jesus Christ who died to finish the work of our liberation over two thousand years ago on the Cross of Calvary.

The third key is to change our paradigm on fixing things and taking responsibility to do something, is to receive His grace with gratitude. Our new paradigm must include an accurate understanding of our world and that we are caught up in the midst of a spiritual war. The war is not arbitrary where only some must participate. It is not pretty and cannot be ultimately ignored or denied.

Finally, we need to repent and cry out to God as Paul did. *"O wretched man that I am, who will deliver me from this Body of Death?"* (Ro. 7:24). We are free to change our minds and stop trying harder to do again and again what we have already done before that has not worked. We have a new option: to seek God and the power of His Word to heal and deliver us.

How Clever Is That?

Even as the war was won on Calvary, it can still be lost in our minds. If the Enemy can successfully recondition us to believe the lies, and we fail to question our circumstances, we will die cooked in his kettle. Like the proverbial frog, we will not even attempt to jump out of the pot. And why is that? Is it for lack of God's direction or is it because the lie, whichever side of wrong it rests on, is easier to believe and far more instant and convenient than the truth? Is the lie that we have been deceived into thinking we feel more comfortable being in control ourselves, even if it is only an illusion?

How will this all end? Simply, just as we would have it! Either God will be God in our lives, or we will be our own gods. Letting go of trying to control things to make them change is trusting in God. Getting better at improving ourselves is an exercise in futility. Let God do the impossible and "perfect that which concerns us," including our deliverance (Ps. 138:8). He is more than willing to finish the work He's begun in us if we just let

Him. "It is finished" (Jn. 19:30). It is His Word, and He does not lie!

"For we are His workmanship created in Christ Jesus unto good works, which God hath before ordained that we should walk in them" (Eph.2:10). Deliverance begins with a cry for help and ends with a call to rest. Rest in the goodness and grace of God, and let Him deliver you from the works of *Darkness* for which you are no match. Amen.

About the Author

M arjorie Cole is the founder of Life Recovery, a prayer counseling ministry, and the author of numerous books on healing and deliverance including *Taking the Devil to Court*. Life Recovery Curriculum offers a wide selection of instruction materials on biblical counseling and spiritual warfare available on her website. She has worked in counseling and deliverance for over twenty-five years. An excellent Bible teacher and conference speaker, Marjorie has traveled both nationally and internationally with her video and audio teachings being seen throughout the world including Africa, Romania, the Middle East, and Europe.

Marjorie has worked as a counselor in both Christian and secular settings. She has a master's degree in Counseling Psychology and Chemical Dependency Counseling, and currently co-hosts a weekly counseling radio talk show, Rescue Radio, with her husband Jarrol, pastor of True Light Church.

Using a biblical approach to counseling and truth as the basis for freedom, Life Recovery presents a systematic, comprehensive approach to healing and deliverance that has helped thousands of people apply scriptural principles to their lives, bringing them to truth and new freedom in Christ. Those principles include understanding spiritual warfare, deliverance, inner healing, breaking generational curses, and discipleship.

Other literary works by Marjorie Cole include *God On Trial—Opening Arguments*, a radio drama series that exposes the war between God and Satan for the souls of men by exploring the question of God's right to rule the world.

See www.liferecovery.com for a complete listing of materials available.

Appendix and Reference Page

Bots
http://www.cisco.com/web/about/security/intelligence/
virusworm-diffs.html

http://justalist.blogspot.com/2008/03/vibrational-fre-
quency-list.html

Electromagnetic Frequencies—The Frequency of the
Human Body ... and Your Coffee. September 17, 2006

https://cellphonesafety.wordpress.com/2006/09/17/
the-frequency-of-the-human-bodyand-your-coffee/

Article printed from Amen Clinics: http://www.amen-
clinics.com/clinics/professionals/howwe-can-help/
brain-science/anterior-cingulate-gyrus-acg/ printpage/
OCD and the Brain—Andrew B. Hollander

http://serendip.brynmawr.edu/bb/neuro/neur000/web1/
Hollander.html

Dan Murphy, DC—Faculty Life Chiropractic College West; Vice President ICA 2003-2009; ICA Chiropractor of the Year 2009

Electromagnetic Charges in Food! By James Spicer | Submitted On August 20, 2008 Article Source:

http://EzineArticles.com/?expert=James_Spicer Article Source: http://EzineArticles.com/1421536

VoiceBio—Frequency & the Body http://www.voicebio.com/ freq-and-body.php

Suggested Materials

You can find these titles and more at www.liferecovery.com.
A Case for Healing (Manual)
Answers to Prayer (CD)
Breaking the Cycle (CD)
Cravings—Why Do I Do What I Don't Want To Do? (2-CD Set)
Eating for Spiritual Health (4-CD Set)
Eating to Live or Living to Eat? (2-CD Set)
If I'm Saved, Why Do I Still Sin? (4-CD Set)
It's My Fault (CD)
Pain & Suffering (CD)
Preparing for Battle (2-CD Set)
Setting Captives Free (Manual)
Spiritual Foundations (2-CD Set)
Taking the Devil to Court (Book)
The Combat Manual
The Truth about Fear, Anxiety, and Panic Attacks (CD)
Trying to Rest (2-CD Set)
Untangling the Lies of the Enemy (2-CD Set)
"Who Am I?" (CD)